W9-BXR-967

On the Client's Path

A MANUAL FOR THE PRACTICE
OF SOLUTION-FOCUSED THERAPY

A. J. Chevalier, Ph.D.

NEW HARBINGER PUBLICATIONS, INC.

Publisher's Note

This publication is designed to provide accurate and authoritative information in regard to the subject matter covered. It is sold with the understanding that the publisher is not engaged in rendering psychological, financial, legal, or other professional services. If expert assistance or counseling is needed, the services of a competent professional should be sought.

Text design by Tracy Marie Powell.
Cover design by SHELBY DESIGNS & ILLUSTRATES.

Distributed in U.S.A. primarily by Publishers Group West; in Canada by Raincoast Books; in Great Britain by Airlift Book Company, Ltd.; in South Africa by Real Books, Ltd.; in Australia by Boobook; and in New Zealand by Tandem Press.

Library of Congress Catalog Card Number: 95-69483

ISBN 1-57224-021-0 hardcover

Printed in the United States of America on recycled paper.

First printing 1995, 3,000 copies

Dedication

To the Great Spirit
in ALL
Who heals us
in our own good time
in our own good way.

Contents

Foreword

On the Client's Path is a simple, straightforward guide to doing better therapy. It is a resource for both the seasoned therapist and the beginning therapist. By using *On the Client's Path*, the therapist cuts through much of the negative history that has too long been a part of the helping professions and moves directly into a positive and solution-oriented approach. By tapping into the innate strengths that all humans possess, the process of therapy is strengthened both in brevity of time and by reducing expenses for the client. At the same time, people empower themselves to solve their own problems.

Ajakai has written a book that can immediately help many different helpers to be more efficient: individual counselors, family therapists, psychologists, school counselors, employee assistance counselors, nurses, teachers, educators, psychiatrists, group leaders, drug and alcohol counselors, and others. It is a book that will help cut through problems and move to the solution. In the process, clients will be helped to feel more competent and more in control of their own lives.

When clients are encouraged to identify strengths and past successes, they immediately begin to think about themselves more positively. They see themselves as possessing strengths, rather than problems, and as being able to cope, rather than being overwhelmed. Although the book is written for the helping professional, in the long run it is likely to prove most useful to their clients. From the experience of working with a professional who uses Solution-Focused Therapy as presented in *On the Client's Path*, clients will be drawn to using the approach in their daily lives.

On the Client's Path is not a book about theories of human development, individual development, or psychology. Nor is it a book about theories of families or theories of family therapy. It is a book about *change*. Because the book is about change, it can be used in many different settings with many different kinds of populations and, most importantly, with many different kinds of problems. It can be used to bring about meaningful change with problems ranging from simple parenting issues, to school conduct disorders, addictive problems such as drug and alcohol addictions, and medical issues. As presented by Ajakai, Solution-Focused Therapy can be used with the many different theories of human development and families and many different counseling approaches.

Ajakai has written a book that should catch on quickly with a diverse group of people working in the helping professions. Both professionals and the general populace are winners from her efforts.

Although I do not know the source of her name, from my experience of working with Ajakai and seeing her use her solution-focused approach in training graduate students in family therapy, community workers, and school counselors, I interpret the name to mean "Justice of the Heart." In twenty-plus years I have never seen any trainer of graduate students create such excitement and growth in students. The ultimate compliment to pay to a trainer is to say "The book is her." Where other authors often lose their way, Ajakai has succeeded. She has found a way to move from the lab setting to the written word and to translate the training process for Solution-Focused Therapy to a book of method. She has succeeded. And all readers of *On the Client's Path* will open themselves to a "new light" or way of thinking about life.

Glen Jennings, Ed.D.
Professor of Family Sciences and Clinic Coordinator
Department of Family Sciences
Texas Woman's University
Denton, Texas

Acknowledgments

This book was written at the urging of numerous students, good friends, and colleagues. I was asked to write what I teach. In doing so, I required many years of student questions, which helped me focus on the power of Solution-Focused Therapy. I required many more years of my own healing and countless moments when I knew I was lost . . . and found the courage to try again.

I am grateful to Insoo Berg, who trusted me to guide my own path and supported my competence whenever she saw it. She caught me doing things well and encouraged me to correct myself.

I am still a student of therapy models and healing traditions. I am guided daily by the traditions of many cultures. In particular, my path has been cleared and illuminated by American Indian colleagues and friends. I found what their ancestors knew. The answers lie in a harmony of oneself with the environment. With them, I have learned to practice loving myself and to tend my healing path. From them, I came to know the power of finding my own wisdom and the power of finding so many ways to heal. I am thankful that the Great Spirit has offered such a bountiful banquet of ways to heal.

This book is a therapy text; at the same time, it speaks of how we walk with each other. Here, we consider what we do with each others' stories. We talk about what we do when another's path is opened to our scrutiny.

I am grateful to Georgia O'Keeffe—from her spirited example I learn to tend the fires on my own path. I am grateful also to my friends, Bill W., and Dr. Bob, whose courage orchestrated fellowships everywhere my path takes me.

The examples of Rosa Parks and Jesse Jackson mean freedom to me. From listening to them, I learned that I have work to do and something to say.

I am fortunate that the "others" in my life were kind to me on my healing journey. They honored me by trusting me to handle my process well. They stood by and watched the wisdom of my path unfold before me like a slow dawn climbing out of the night sky.

These others held lanterns that lighted my path: Glen Jennings, Jeff Tiebout, Martha Goller, Marilyn Lichtman and Martin Gerstein, Bud Protinsky, Pam Rogers and Sue Tarr, Marie Draudt, Linda Brock, Lillian Chenoweth, Jan Martin Dunn, Mary Becceril, Jim Petitt, Bill Summy, Carl Bennett, Colleen Johnson, Gail Vargo, Jack Cockburn, Mike Frazier, Lynn and Don Kemerait, Kathie Carlson, Clarissa Pinkola-Estes, Emu, Dolly Jenkins, Jolynne Reynolds, Gladys Hildreth, Bea Lovejoy, Billy Rogers, Silo Black Crow, Mary Helen Deer Smith, Terri McGrath, Bernadette Facundo, Cynthia Alcoze, Charles Battiest, Bette Lynn Paez, Lin Hui-ling, Chang Hung Hsiu, Mary Jane Cimino, Mary Graves, Mary Richey, Keith and Amy Cendrick, Ron and Joy Hickman,

Judah, Robert Big Elk, Aja Sunn, Tsultrim Allione, five gals in the sky, and the folks at Al-Anon.

What a company of lanterns!

And to . . .

Kay, Bill, and Barcus Brooks, who kept my home fires burning and the path well-lit. In order to do good therapy, I found with them the courage to want to heal myself first. It is with their courage that mine has grown.

And to the clients I have known

You make me think

About my work

And me

You are still my Light in the Darkness.

Introduction

This book is a practical interpretation of Solution-Focused Therapy. It comes about after six years of watching the experts do this therapy, of thinking about each aspect of the model, and, most importantly, of seriously considering the questions my students have asked. Through conversations with students and with clients, I sensed a need to construct a "formula" for doing this kind of therapy. As Steve deShazer studied Milton Erickson's work for patterns, I studied deShazer's and Insoo Berg's work for a "recipe" or formula that could be followed on most occasions and applied to most human problems. I spent countless hours observing the therapy teams of the Brief Family Therapy Center in Milwaukee, Wisconsin, as they worked. The results are presented here for the benefit of therapists, their teachers, and their clients.

In their work, most helpers find themselves wearing many hats, with little time to change from one role to the next. Accordingly, the formula is presented in two forms: one using a fifty-minute format, and a second using a twenty-minute format. Although the formula is essentially the same for both formats, the techniques for its use differ due to the amount of available time. These different techniques are offered to meet the demands of helping persons in many situations and professional environments: medical clinics, school settings, employment interviews, inpatient and outpatient facilities, and the like.

In addition to limited time frames and resources, many helpers are also expected to function with limited training or access to training. If you currently work under conditions like these, this book was written with you in mind. It is not necessary to hold advanced educational degrees to use the model of therapy presented here. It is helpful to be a good listener, and, more importantly, to be willing to be taught about life by the clients who tell you their stories. It is equally important to be able to set yourself and your personal business aside to visit in the world of the client. These basic counseling skills provide the foundation for doing this work well. If the formula is followed and these skills are added to it, good results can be expected.

Solution-Focused Therapy

Solution-Focused Therapy is a goal-oriented therapy. For the most part, clients set measurable goals and meet these goals in a timely fashion (usually eight sessions or less, although more sessions can be added if needed).

This therapy sees clients as powerful agents of change who come to therapy with all that they need to correct and heal themselves. Clients are viewed as ever-changing and capable of making any needed change; the therapist expects, watches for, and highlights any change that reaches toward the stated goal.

The solution-focused approach is a nondirective one that relies on the client's own perception of the problem. The focus is on the present and the future, as the therapist searches for what is good and useful that the client has done or is doing to find a solution. The client is left in charge of the healing process, and the therapist trusts that healing will occur at the right time and in the right way. The "right way" is seen as the solution that fits the client's perception of what is right for his or her path at this particular time.

Sessions provide a safe and powerful context for change. This context is built on the interaction between client and therapist, as clients tell their stories and the therapist listens and responds with a number of solution-focused questions.

The telling of one's own story is an age-old healing tradition. In Solution Focused Therapy, the therapist's response maintains a necessary balance between listening and questioning that comes as a result of practice. Moreover, the interaction between client and therapist is based on a mutual respect—a respect that begins with the first contact with the client and proceeds to the end of the therapy.

When respect, listening, and good questions are balanced, the change that results is frequently profound and often comes quickly. Everyone recognizes the change. It is obvious. It moves quickly into the life of the client and settles there, accompanied by an increased sense of self-esteem and empowerment on the client's part. The change lasts over time and affects other parts of the client's life. The change is what the client wanted, and therapy is a success.

This approach is profoundly different from the belief that therapy is a one-way street, a one-sided transfer of insight from helper to client. Here, therapy is viewed as an exchange, and the healing that results is seen as a joint construction.

While clients may try to attribute their changes to us, as therapists we have come to recognize that we have simply linked whatever healing skills we have with the natural healing capacity that exists within them. It is a dance we do together. They lead and we learn to follow. In the end, they tell us that they have grown, and we find that we have grown with them.

What the Reader Can Expect

From reading this book and practicing Solution-Focused Therapy, the reader can expect to:

1. Learn a systematic way of doing therapy that produces satisfying results.

2. See real connections between what the therapist does in the therapy room and client progress.

3. Learn how to help any client set a reachable therapy goal.

4. Gain practice in identifying client strengths and putting these to work.

5. Learn how to create a context where client competence is promoted and client successes are highlighted and maintained.

6. Learn techniques to honor differences among people and recognize a role for the therapist that is not intrusive for the client's process.

7. Develop a sense of the personal healing strengths and the self-corrective capacities that all humans share.

8. Appreciate and use counseling skills already acquired and develop a new sense of your "observing self" as the therapist in the therapy experience.

9. Find a way to enjoy doing therapy and have energy left over at the end of the day for your personal life.

10. Witness profound change often.

The first six of these are skills from which clients directly benefit. Students of therapy and those already in clinical practice will find that these skills make it possible for therapy to proceed faster and for change to be realized sooner than expected.

Moreover, clients will feel the safety of a context that respects their points of view and puts their strengths to work. In this context, they learn to recognize when it is time to do the work on their own. This is a natural restorative process.

These benefits are often felt immediately by the clients. Some client responses are muffled by tears—tears that indicate that a deep chord has been struck and the client feels understood. Other thoughts that they express clearly reflect the impact of being heard and having their personal strengths valued and praised:

"I've never had anyone tell me I was doing well."

"We think we are approaching normal."

"I think I've gotten what I needed out therapy."

"I can handle it the rest of the way myself."

"This is the first time anyone has listened to what I think."

"I think you really understand me."

"We'll see you next time to tell you what we are doing that works for us."

"You are the only one who has ever seen how hard I tried."

"You know what this means to me."

"How did you know how I feel?"

Therapy experienced this way has enduring residual effects. Perhaps, over time, these residual effects become part of the natural healing core that helps anyone thrive. Whatever the explanation for lasting change and increased self-esteem, the client reaches the stated goal and gains a new self-perception. By definition, then, therapy is successful.

The final four benefits are for therapists. Student therapists often report feeling a new excitement about their work with clients when using this therapy. Witnessing moments of change in session has a profound influence on therapists. The most profound effect seems to be in the area of gaining respect for each client and for human strength in general. In moments of jubilation when a client unties a personal knot comes an abiding sense of gratitude for being given the experience of sharing another's world.

What the Reader Will Find in This Book

On the Client's Path begins with two chapters covering the basic counseling skills and theoretical premises underlying this model of therapy. The reader is offered a brief encounter with ideas about the nature of change, listening, getting client cooperation, client strength, and the nature of problem solving.

Chapter 3 begins coverage of the techniques of the solution-focused model with discussion of the first part of the formula for a written intervention: gaining client cooperation by paying careful attention to client language and affect. In this book, this strategy is called "accessing the client view." It forms the basis of maintaining client motivation and cooperation during the entire course of therapy.

Chapter 4 covers the importance of setting a goal for therapy, and questions to help the client do so are presented.

The second component of the formula for intervention is identification of client strengths. Chapter 5 covers techniques for searching out strengths and for presenting these strengths to clients in the form of compliments that they can recognize as true about themselves.

The final component of the formula for intervention involves a search for "exceptions": times when the client's problem is somehow different. Something that the client has done or noticed has made this difference, and it is in this variance that hope for a solution can be found. Chapter 6 covers the search for exceptions to the problem situation.

In chapter 7, the components of the intervention come together in a formula for a written intervention that can be used repeatedly in every session and with each new client. The format for writing this intervention is presented and discussed, together with suggestions for taking notes during the session that will aid the writing of the intervention.

Chapter 8 summarizes the processes of the first seven chapters and presents a scheme for thinking about the path to solutions in each session. The structure of both long-format and short-format sessions is outlined, together with suggestions for therapists working alone or with therapy teams and a description of a solution-focused case-presentation format.

Chapter 9 focuses on techniques to mark improvement and to note and encourage success. Chapter 10 presents special strategies for working with clients who are experiencing "worst-case" situations or are just barely getting by. Chapter 11 offers specific strategies for emergencies and urgent problems such as suicide, addictions, and sexual abuse.

Chapter 12 covers the specifics of the twenty-minute interview format in the form of a pattern of questions that can be used in every session. Questions are given for the client who is self-referred and for involuntary clients, along with a companion interview format for the referring person that can be done over the phone.

Chapter 13 outlines applications of the solution-focused approach in a variety of other settings, including medical clinics, schools, college counseling centers, and employment interviews. Strategies are also discussed for parents who wish to adapt solution-focused concepts for use with their children.

One Last Word

This text is my view of how Solution-Focused Therapy works, based on my observation of experts, my own work, and my students' work over a six-year period. My greatest teachers, though, have been the clients themselves—hundreds of them, from ethnically diverse backgrounds, and exquisite teachers all. I owe a huge debt of understanding to these courageous individuals for sharing their stories with me and inviting me to watch them grow. This work is offered in the hope that more therapists will come to view their clients as the wise and powerful beings that all of us are.

1

About Wisdom, Honor, and Respect

All of life—every living thing is pulsating with medicine—every rock, plant, river has healing power.

Ortiz and Erdoes

Persons carry inner wisdom, their very own power to heal.

Wisdom, honor, and respect: What do these words mean to us as therapists?

What is needed to see the wisdom of others? (Do others really know what is best for their own lives?) What does it mean to honor others and what we see in their life experiences? What does it mean to respect another's point of view?

Wisdom, we are told by the *American Heritage Dictionary*, is the "understanding of what is true, right, or lasting." It is common sense, good judgment, or one's learning. Learning, we know, comes from the accumulation of life's experiences, whether these experiences occur in a formal classroom or in our daily lives.

Honor, according to the *American Heritage Dictionary*, is the "action of holding in respect, esteem; to show respect for, to place distinction upon, to accept as valid."

Respect, according to the same source, is the "action of showing or feeling courteous regard for; showing deference; courteous yielding to the wishes, judgment, or opinion of another; avoiding violation of or interference with."

The meanings of the last two words are nearly interchangeable. They are the basis for good therapeutic relationships.

Many models of counseling use different terms for these same concepts—"unconditional positive regard" is a familiar formula. Here, these concepts imply that some things will be done: the beholder, in this case a therapist, will show respect for or accept as valid that which he or she observes. There is also the implication that other things will not be done: the therapist will avoid violating or interfering with the client's current thinking.

What does it take to visit a client's world without judging what we find there? When someone is vastly different from ourselves, how can we approach those differences in a way that honors what we hear? And if we do find a way to suspend judgment on what we find in a client's world, a way to respect the reality of his or her point of view, how will that approach affect the therapeutic relationship?

This text outlines techniques for putting these concepts into practice. They are techniques for showing respect and honoring what is brought by any client.

Acts that honor and respect set the stage for cooperation. Clients want to participate in healing endeavors when their opinions and wishes are held in high regard by the helping person. Since they often enter therapy with very different expectations, acts of esteem and courtesy may come as a pleasant and somewhat unsettling surprise. Whatever the reaction, it comes in response to a gentle invitation to enter into a healing event. Such acts call forth the client's natural healing capacity.

Honor and respect lead clients to experience the therapist as being "easy to talk to," "trustworthy," and "comfortable to be with." Therapy becomes an engaging affair. Clients look forward to it and actively pursue their chosen goals. They return for the second, third, and fourth sessions. They finish the work they came to do.

These techniques are designed to result in a therapeutic practice that avoids interference and holds the client's experience in high esteem—regardless of his or her station in life. These simple acts are often hard ones for a therapist to perform. All too quickly, we lose our willingness to understand what has brought a client to a particular belief or set of circumstances. We are off without a thought to the secure and comforting walls of our own beliefs and experience. From there, we offer advice that fits our world, or we throw stones at a world we refuse to understand—or we do both.

From this vantage point, we are willing and able to offer the "help" of reconstructing another's life. We forget that others too are comforted by their own beliefs; they have lenses of their own through which they see life. And their beliefs offer them as much comfort as ours offer us.

As therapists, few of us were trained to be companions in the process of healing. We often prefer the role of guide in others' territories, even when we are unsure of the shape or composition of their terrain. We feel that we know our clients' territory by looking at our own maps.

Beliefs have a peculiar holding power; we all cling to the comfort of our beliefs as we would wrap ourselves up in a heavy coat in a blizzard. When therapists offer their beliefs as *the* way to look at things, we lose any possible connection with the client and at the same time lose his or her cooperation. Then, of course, we are prone to ask why. What happened to the client that she or he no longer wants to take part in therapy?

Choosing our view over the client's view renders the client invisible. In many cases this is a frightening outcome, especially if clients are coming to therapy to become more visible to themselves and others.

Honoring means showing reverence for the human condition and esteem for the person in it. Similarly, respect means deferring or yielding to the opinion or viewpoint of another. In my work, this has meant regarding the client as the expert on his or her own life and accepting the validity of his or her opinions about it. It has also meant working from the position that clients are changing right before my eyes. Given a context of support and encouragement, they will make the adjustments that they need to make. I wait and watch for these changes.

Having read all this, you ask, "What happens to *my* opinion?" My response is "Whose session is it?" If the session truly does belong to the client, then the therapist's opinion must be secondary to the client's view. The therapist is a visitor and a guest in the client's world. The therapist's job there is to illuminate the parts of that world that the client brings to the table for discussion. The job is to search for strength in the midst of turmoil and not to rearrange client perceptions.

In the client's world, the scenery may be very different from the scenery in my own. It is my role to be in this strange place without rearranging it and without doing harm to it. As a guest, it is my role to act in a way that enhances what is already there and to watch the client do the rearranging. This, I think, is the context for the emergence of client wisdom.

A safe, appreciative context opens the door to a healing force, the force found in all of us. Such a context sends a strong message to those coming for help: "What you bring is all you need!"

Building a Context for Client Wisdom

What behaviors support a visit to the client's world?

Those of you who are field veterans already know them. They are those familiar verbal and nonverbal signals that you use to let clients know that they have found a safe place to do their work and a safe helper to invite on this leg of their life's journey. Consider what follows a chance to revisit moments of your training for a quick "checkup."

For others new to the practice of therapy, or who have found themselves working in the field without prior knowledge or training, much of what follows may be new information. Detailed coverage of the supportive and nonsupportive helping behaviors outlined here can be found in Barbara Okun's 1982 book, *Effective Helping*.

Supportive verbal behaviors. Okun lists the following basic supportive verbal behaviors: using understandable words, reflecting back to the clients what has been said, clarifying client ideas, and using verbal reinforcers such as "I see" or "yes." She notes that clients also value the occasional use of humor to reduce tension and feel supported when therapists request feedback from them. She recommends addressing the client by first name or as "you." She states that appropriate interpretation is important, as is suspending personal judgement of a client's situation or options in that situation.

Used in a cohesive fashion, which requires much practice over time, these skills beckon the client to invite the helper in for a closer look at her or his world. These skills send a signal that the helper is interested, listening, and paying close attention to what is so important to the client.

Supportive nonverbal behaviors. Nonverbal skills are the vehicles by which the verbal skills travel. The two need to match. When they carry different messages, the client becomes focused on what is going on with the helper—the exact reverse of what the therapy situation sets out to be. Nonverbal cues include tone of voice, eye contact, head movement, facial animation and expression, rate of speech, physical distance, and body language.

Specifically, the therapist's tone of voice should be similar to that of the client. There should also be appropriate eye contact, meaning that the therapist matches what the client is doing with his or her eyes. Bear in mind that the kind of eye contact that one culture or individual views as a sign of interest or attention may seem like a rude stare or a mark of disrespect to another. Rather than impose his or her personal beliefs, here again the therapist should simply follow the client's lead.

Nods of the head and animated facial expressions can both communicate an interest in the client's topic. Yet both should also be regulated, in order to avoid communicating judgment of an action or investment in a particular stance that the client may have taken.

Occasional smiles and humor and the use of hand gestures and body language should again match the client's use of these. This is not to say that the therapist should simply parrot or mimic clients' behavior. Rather, a careful attempt to match the nonverbal cues that clients give is made, in an effort to honor their stance on any issue. My experience has been that validating the client view in this way leads to cooperation and minimizes resistance.

I have found that an appropriate physical distance of around 39 inches usually sets up a comfortable setting. Once again, it is useful to recognize that different cultural orientations have different expectations in this area. Most clients are willing to advise when asked if they are comfortable with seating arrangements.

Physical touch is infrequently used in Solution-Focused Therapy, and it is regarded with special caution when the client's presenting problem is related to physical touch. The profession's ethical standards are the basic guidelines. For my part, I avoid making my own attitudes an issue, and I am willing to question them if the client's behavior suggests that I can safely do so. I am careful to keep my behavior within limits that do not confuse the client. If I hug a client, it is clear to both of us that it is all right for me to do so.

Nonsupportive behaviors. Most clients are very attentive readers of the verbal and nonverbal behaviors of the helper, and they use the cues they find to come up with their own reading of how helpful the helper can actually be. They watch for and often expect what Okun calls "nonsupportive behaviors." These include advice giving, preaching, placating, blaming, cajoling, exhorting, or directing. Using big words, asking too many probing questions, giving too many interpretations, and generally presenting an attitude that says "I know what is best for you" are sure ways to end the therapy process. While clients usually expect the helper to offer direction, too much self-disclosure and too many answers are disruptive to the process.

Okun also lists nonverbal behaviors that are nonsupportive. These include inappropriate physical distance, frowning, no facial animation, yawning, closed eyes or poor eye contact, distracting behaviors, and an inappropriate rate of speech. When clients experience any of these behaviors in the helper, alone or in combination, they are distracted from their own process. Their own process is the business of the therapy hour. It is the work to be done.

Confidentiality

Likewise, helpers need to pay particular attention to the issue of confidentiality. To begin with, the setting for the therapy needs to be private, quiet, and without interruption. Beyond that, clients usually require assurance that the helpers regard their personal material as private and not for the eyes and ears of others. Since this is a crucial concern, I state how confidentiality will be handled at the first session.

I share information about clients with their signed written consent. When another agency or a court requests information, I share only the information that is requested, and not the client's entire history. A copy of what is shared is made available to the client at his or her request.

Other situations where information is shared about a client include times when the client is a threat to self or others. Clients are informed of these procedures as part of our introduction to one another. I am careful to answer specific questions about procedures promptly anytime they arise in the course of therapy and to provide answers that resolve the questions or concerns important to the client. Concerns like these arise as part of the healing process.

Use of Videotape, Audiotape, Therapy Teams, and Observation

In many therapy situations, helpers are now videotaping or audiotaping sessions, observing live sessions, or using a therapy team behind a one-way mirror. All of these practices are potent teaching tools and serve to make better therapy and therapists.

When a session will be taped, I say the following to my clients:

> I would like to videotape our work today. Only my supervisor will
> view this tape. I want to make sure that I am serving you well, and my
> supervisor will be commenting on how well I served you. I will tape
> over the used portion of this tape after the supervisor has viewed it. Do
> you have any concerns about this or questions you would like to ask?

If I am fortunate enough to have a team and a one-way mirror available, I say this:

> Today we have a team of therapists ready to help you. They are
> students *(or counselors)* like me and their job is to make sure I do a good
> job for you. They are there to evaluate me, not you. What questions do
> you have about this? Do you have any concerns about this that I need
> to know before we proceed?

Case Note

"I'm not sure I can talk." *A young man in his twenties was referred to me for counseling regarding his stated wish to commit suicide. He had never been to a counselor before and stated up front his concern that he might know the team members or that some of them might know him. Here is a segment of that interview:*

Cliff: I'm not sure I can talk in front of a lot of people. I don't really want to be around anyone, specially with this problem. They probably know me.

Therapist: Their job is to watch me, and as counselors their job is to make sure I do a good job for you.

Cliff: What's going on with me is so big that I can't handle it anymore. Something has to be done.

Therapist: They are bound by the laws of this state to keep what they hear private and confidential. The tape is for me to review only, and I destroy it after I have studied it.

Cliff: I need a lot of help with this or I am not going to make it through the next few days.

Therapist: The job you and I have to do is a big one, right?

Cliff (shaking his head): You don't know the half of it.

Therapist: How would it be to have six counselors helping you with this big a problem? Would that work? I mean, if we all work on it together, would that be enough help?

Cliff: Yes.

In this case, Cliff was nervous about the team and about being observed as well as about coming to a counselor for the first time. I answered his questions and used his concern about the size of his problem to get cooperation. I also set his mind at ease when I told him that the team was watching me to make sure that I did a good job for him. I made a mental note of his concern about privacy and kept that in my mind throughout the course of therapy.

In any case, if clients insist that they do not want to be taped or observed, I yield to their beliefs and work without taping or observation. I use signed consent forms for taping and observation for those who are willing.

Clinical Supervision and Formal Training

It has been my experience that new therapists grow immensely both from supervision with an established licensed professional and from formal academic training. If therapists have not had much formal training and are expected to see clients, I ask that they insist on support from their agencies to receive formal training. While this may seem like an obvious point, a number of managers in human service settings do not recognize it or place a high priority on the in-service needs of their therapists.

A good training package consists of formal training and ongoing clinical supervision with an established clinical supervisor. The supervisor's approach to therapy and supervision should both match the training needs of the agency seeking his or her services. The fit is ultimately determined by the agency. A contract between the two can address these needs and assure that they will be met.

Beyond the Basics

These basics form the foundation for any helping context. Supportive verbal and non-verbal behaviors make the setting conducive to talk about private matters and painful issues. A clear agreement between therapist and client about the nature of their relationship and its setting likewise provides a context for therapeutic work. These basic helping skills are all prerequisites for practicing Solution-Focused Therapy.

What lies beyond these basics is the therapist's own curiosity about the human condition and his or her ability to listen with the ears and with the heart. I listen for what is being said and what is not being said. My attention sharpens as clients go deeper into their stories and begin to face the scary places. The therapist's job remains the same throughout therapy, to go to the scary places with our clients, careful always to illuminate their strengths and help bring the challenges they face into focus.

Veteran therapists who know and operate from other models of therapy will recognize useful intersections between Solution-Focused Therapy and the models they use. Noteworthy connections have already been made with Rational Emotive Therapy, Reality Therapy, cognitive behaviorist styles, strategic therapies, family-of-origin approaches, behavior modification, twelve-step addiction concepts, Rogerian work, and Jungian analysis. You may find it useful to interweave the therapy models that you know well with this new model. Or you may feel ready to set aside the models that you know best for an adventure with a new approach, returning later to blend useful skills from each into a unique style.

In my own work, I have found it natural to adopt a blend of Jungian work and Solution-Focused Therapy concepts. This blend gives me the ability to work either on a long-term or a short-term basis and to use all the bits and pieces of clients' lives and stories in therapy, including dreams, symbols, archetypal images, and the meanings given to these by clients' subconscious minds.

"Doing Is Knowing"

I assume that each of us is about the business of developing a unique style. I also assume that this style comes about only after much practice and experience—both as a helper and as a recipient of the therapy process. It takes courage to heal, no matter who is doing it; when we know that courage firsthand, we signal our clients that we are also human, and that signal is as clear to them as a neon light. It tells them that their process is just as "doable," at a time when many of them are questioning the very possibility of change in their lives.

"Doing is knowing," Insoo Berg writes about clinical supervision. Likewise, doing personal healing work means knowing what it takes to do that work and finding out about the courage that is needed to live through real personal change. As a therapist, it means knowing what your own issues are and making a commitment to yourself to work on them. It is knowing that you have not arrived and that you are no different from those who come for your help. The healthy therapist is one who knows that he or she has issues to resolve and who works on them as a way of life.

A Curiosity That Holds Respect

The components discussed here are the initial steps we take toward finding our own wisdom. Another essential element in this work is *a curiosity that holds respect* (Bennett 1993). This curiosity is the element that keeps the therapist attentive to each word from a client. The respect that it holds is in turn a collection of actions that the therapist does as these are interpreted by clients. If clients were asked about their experience with a therapist whose practice incorporates this element, each of them would readily say, "I feel understood."

Beyond these elements, are hearts that knew wounding and endured anyway. This endurance was due to an unquenchable desire—a universal hope to be healthier, happier humans—and a speck of internal wisdom that guided each of us, no matter what we faced.

Yet finding our way down the path of wisdom requires something more. It is not enough to suspend judgment and validate the client's experience. The therapy needs to move toward a goal—at the client's pace and in the client's own manner, with small successes marked along the way. For these efforts, more specific techniques are needed. The next five chapters will cover these techniques for moving the therapy forward, with curiosity and respect, toward client goals.

2

Premises of Solution-Focused Therapy

What we think about lives and ourselves determines much of what happens to us.

Norman Vincent Peale

What we think about what we think may be better than the original thought.

The theoretical basis for Solution-Focused Therapy could be called *phenomenological*, in the sense that it begins with a picture of human awareness that emphasizes our ability to make meaning out of our experiences. In part, this emphasis represents a simple acknowledgment that the personal interpretation we give to any experience is supremely important to each of us. In a deeper sense, the underlying premise of the solution-focused approach is that the ability to make meaning is crucial to our very existence. It is certainly crucial to the practice of this therapy.

The link between survival and this ability to make meaning out of even the most horrible circumstances is particularly evident during a crisis. When we detach ourselves from a situation and choose a meaning for it, we then develop strategies to cope with it or start to move toward a resolution.

What we find then is that the meaning selected for any given human situation becomes as important as the impact of the original event in the person's life. We become very attached to the meanings that we have selected. In some ways, the meaning an individual gives to a situation is much like a painting, created from brush strokes of words and given a character as unique as the person who created it.

Over a lifetime, the meanings that each of us select are likely to follow a predictable path. In responding to the countless events that we experience, we rely on a limited number of interpretations to organize those events, and these interpretations form a recognizable pattern. Usually we are unaware of this pattern, even though others can often see parts of it quite clearly, and many of its aspects may be readily visible to the careful attention of a concerned helper.

One of the peculiarities of this experience is that each of us regards our own map as "the Truth." If the details of our pattern are challenged, each of us defends *the* map we *know* to be true.

Out of the thousands of possible meanings any given situation could have, the one we select matches the internal map we have selected. The map is a lifelong accumulation of experience and interpretations of these experiences, and the experiences of a lifetime are hard to set aside. We may offer these interpretations as opinions, but to a greater or a lesser degree we tend to see them as fact. To a greater or a lesser extent we try to impose our interpretations on others, and we are more or less successful in doing so. In therapy, persuasion is often a very tough game to play.

However we view our own interpretations, whether we see them as personal opinion or as absolute truth, two things remain true for all humans: (1) It is often *very* difficult to change someone's interpretation, and (2) everyone's interpretation is vitally important to them. We usually notice both of these characteristics whenever we attempt to change someone else's opinion. A verbal wrestling match begins!

Because we all share this same mechanism, it follows that the decisions we make are based on the knowledge *and* the understanding that we have at any given time. A friend once said to me that we always make the best decision we can at any moment—given the light we had at that moment on the subject at hand. As therapists, when we understand that people are doing the best they can in any given circumstance, then we can begin to free ourselves from our own judgment and start to really listen to what our clients are saying to us.

As we listen carefully, we hear the "facts" of personal situations. These facts are explanations of events. Sometimes they are offered in the barest of words; at others times we hear more elaborate accounts, and often metaphors. One client told me that her husband left "like a cat in the night." Her description of this event was like a brush stroke on a painting—unique and painfully hers. It colored her situation for me in a particular way. It helped me to understand her view by looking closely at the picture her words made.

Her word picture is *not* the sum total of her life experience, nor is it her person. It is merely one representation of her experience—perhaps the nearest in time or the closest in feeling at this moment, but not the only one. To think otherwise is the same as confusing an artist with her latest painting. We can appreciate her latest work and still know that she can create very different pictures if she chooses. Our clients too are more than the sum total of any of their words.

When I make the choice to respect another's internal map, wonderful things begin to happen. More often than not, the respect is returned and cooperation becomes the norm for how we get along. A standard is set for how to conduct the therapy.

Choosing to realize that people are still influenced by their past experiences means accepting each individual as the "expert" of his or her situation. Respect for each expert means that I validate the experiences and responses to those experiences that each has had. I meet them at the door of their worlds, willing to walk through and see what is there with them as my guides.

Accepting the client's interpretation of an experience also means accepting the ways the client chooses to explain it to me. If I choose to respect all the messages that the client offers, the client feels more willing to share and to cooperate with my suggestions. The setting itself becomes an affirming one that the client recognizes as safe and nurturing. Such a setting makes it highly likely that the client will return to complete the therapy.

Similarly, I choose to view clients as strong persons, capable of making the changes that they need to make. I view them as having had successes in the past, and I look diligently for those successes that will help with the current problem they are facing. After all, we humans are a resourceful species, and that resourcefulness is shared by clients and therapists alike.

I see clients as persons with choices: my job is to help them clarify what those choices are. I view humans as adept at making choices and as capable of using good choices they have made in the past to help them today.

I assume that clients make choices that match how they interpret their situations. These choices allow them to feel psychologically comfortable. What makes one comfortable is likely to be done again and again.

When clients come for help, their focus is their current dilemma. That is what brought them to therapy, and I stay with that focus. My view is that asking about past successes is a way of helping both of us sharpen that focus, and I continue to do so, even if previous accomplishments seem very meager.

Often, the problems clients bring are complex and can seem overwhelming to them. It is useful to break the problem down into smaller pieces and work on these pieces until success in one area is realized. Success in one small area seems to breed success in other areas. Clients benefit from experiencing success and feel encouraged to move on to tackle other issues.

I assume that people are always responding; even silence is a response. I tune into the client's responses and keep running mental notes of how they respond in order to update my sense of how they picture their situations.

Finally, I assume that no behavior or human response exists in a vacuum. Rather, each of us is an interactive part of the system of relationships in which we live. Any change in the ways we relate to one another creates a possibility for significant change in our system of relationships. I see the greatest potential for change coming from the person who is the most flexible in any relationship. This person is usually more likely to possess a range of behaviors and responses.

These ideas are far from new; for me, their origin was an encounter with *The Answer Within*, by Stephen and Carol Lankton. Indeed, the title of that book describes an experience that I have witnessed countless times, as a client and as a therapist, in working with students and in my own work. *The answers are generated within.* My clients have shown me that this is so, and I have seen my students find ways to correct themselves as well.

The answers are generated within, and they appear in a context of relationships that help us to prepare for them and adjust to accommodate their arrival. Clients find answers within when they work on their problems in a nurturing atmosphere where they are encouraged to take responsibility for their own growth and change. Such an atmosphere occurs when we accept the idea that each of us has the ability to change in the ways that we need to change. All humans can heal; all humans carry a source of healing power and healing wisdom within.

Basic Premises of Solution-Focused Therapy

From the work that I observed and participated in at the Brief Family Therapy Center, I learned the value of exploring the beliefs that form the basis of any therapy. As therapists, we usually practice a model of therapy whose beliefs closely match our own. Often we are unaware of just how influential these beliefs are in determining what we choose to do as therapists.

The premises or underlying beliefs of Solution-Focused Therapy offered here were related by the staff of the Brief Family Therapy Center. It is important to recognize that they are beliefs or premises, not truths. The point of examining them is not to establish a "right" or "wrong" way of doing therapy, but to clarify the differences between the approaches we take and to examine their implications for our clients.

1. It is easier to build on strengths and past successes than to try to correct past failures or mistakes. My experience has been that taking this path offers a pleasant journey for both client and therapist. At first, clients may be a bit surprised at my interest in what's going well with them in relation to the problem at hand. Part of the suprise is that few of us expect to focus on what is going well at a time when our lives have grown difficult enough to drive us into therapy. Praise can also produce a kind of cultural shock: our society is so fascinated with all that is negative that clients are often startled to meet someone who insists on pointing out how good or promising something they are doing is. For many clients, an even more important part of the surprise is the realization that some progress has already been or can soon be made.

In any case, clients are usually intrigued by therapists who watch for their strengths, and therapy that focuses on strengths has a magnetic appeal for them. Quite simply, each of us likes to be caught doing something well.

2. If we listen closely, clients will tell us how to cooperate with them. Essentially, clients tell us how they see themselves and invite us to see them that way as well. They tell us what is important to them, and they want us to understand their view of their problem. When we "get it" and can demonstrate to them that we have heard what they are saying, they feel understood.

One of my clients instructed me and our team to hold back on compliments when she did things well; our praise, she thought, would surely cause her next failure. While some therapists would have explored this "resistance" to technique, I concluded that she was wise to refuse compliments. The team and I did what we were told to do and held back our compliments until she felt comfortable enough with her progress to tell us that it was all right to compliment her again.

An 82-year-old client had been "jailed" at the local nursing home for slapping his wife of 54 years; since he did not remember this event, he considered himself innocent of the charge. When he was referred to me for counseling, he relayed this remark through the home's social worker: "I've never needed a counselor in 82 years and I'm not going now!" With her help, I replied with this message: "Of course, you have never needed a counselor, so why would you come to one now?"

His reply came back to me through the social worker: "Well, I'm not seeing any counselor in my room!" Again, my response to him took his feelings into account: "Of course, you're not seeing any counselor in your room!"

We continued our correspondence through a further round. His next exchange was: "Well, I'm not seeing any counselor alone! I want my attorney present, especially if it's a woman. You know how women are!" My response again incorporated his feelings, which were justly his, based on his life experience. My reply was: "What a good idea! Please call your attorney and ask him to sit in on this session. And I certainly do know how women are!"

The outcome of this flurry of messages was that he gave me his full cooperation. Without having seen me, his experience of me was that I understood his view of things and that he could trust that understanding enough to talk to me. I had honored him by listening to what was important to him and taking its importance seriously; he responded by trusting me and taking what went on in our session with equal seriousness.

3. Preconceptions about clients hamper the therapist and prevent a flexible use of technique. The messages that the social worker relayed to me from my nursing home client could have been interpreted in a number of ways. If I had simply made up my mind that he was "uncooperative" or "hostile" or "tough to deal with," then that is all he would have turned out to be, and I would probably not have talked to him at all. In avoiding any preconceived notions about this man, my only conviction was that his viewpoint was real for him and that by expressing it he was telling me how to cooperate with him. When I did so, the result for him was that there was no one there for him to fight or "resist," and so he chose to talk to me and went on to sign up for another session.

4. Insight or awareness is not always necessary for change to occur; insight may occur before or after a change in behavior. Considering what happens to people when they try to diet is a helpful way of thinking about this premise. Even though we may know *why* we eat and gain weight, that knowledge does not always change *how* or *what* or *when* we eat or other eating behaviors that we would like to change. I have found it helpful to ask "Why?" questions or to focus on gaining insights when this kind of awareness is the client's goal in therapy or when the client thinks that insight will help to solve a current problem. When those indications are not present, I stick with efforts to meet the goal that the client has chosen for therapy.

5. Symptoms are not necessarily the expression of underlying past traumas, problems, or character weaknesses. At some level, most symptoms are probably related to past traumas or problems, yet it is time consuming to search for prior causes and often difficult to demonstrate the relevance of these conclusions. I have found it more helpful to focus on a present goal and only search for a connection to the past when clients think that this is a good idea. Here again, take their assessment of the current situation into account and take directions from them on how to proceed. The resources that clients have in terms of time, money, and energy are also a relevant consideration; if clients are depending on insurance to help cover the cost of therapy work, then the opportunity to manage these resources needs to be offered, and focusing on a specific goal will help us move toward the desired outcome in a timely manner.

6. All parts of a system are interrelated and interconnected. When I work with clients, I become part of the matrix of human relationships that serves as a host to the current problem they are facing. This human ecosystem influences their thoughts, feelings, and behaviors, and they, in turn, influence the system in which they find themselves. Since a change in one part of a client's system creates a potential for change in each of its other parts, accepting the complexity of this environment is an essential basis of therapeutic work.

A corollary of this premise is that the therapist need not distrust clients' descriptions of their problems or relationships or spend time trying to persuade clients to bring others from their matrix into therapy. I accept whoever shows up with the thought that the individual that the client's system selected for me to work with must be the best candidate. Trusting that selection process is part of trusting client wisdom.

7. It is difficult to know if there are clear causes and effects in human relationships. The complexity of human relationships makes it extremely difficult to say with certainty that one event caused another or that one set of events produced another set. The search for causes can become an endless chase, and the client's goal may be lost in the process. Again, I only make an effort to search for causes when clients wish to focus on the past or think that it will help to solve a current dilemma.

8. Change is constant and inevitable. Our task as therapists is to help clients bring about positive change. I view clients as I do other natural systems; they are caught in a tension between changing and staying the same. I find it helpful to remember that change happens all the time, even though the increments may be small ones and not always noticeable to the client or to an outside observer. Think of the small change that happens when you wash your face in the morning: you lose traces of dead skin, although you still recognize yourself when you look in the mirror. I remind myself that change is happening and that I can expect it to occur. Watching closely, I will see it soon.

9. Small changes lead to bigger changes. Each client has his or her own pace. Some move ahead very slowly at first and then, without warning, make a number of rapid moves to solve their own problems. Others take fast first steps and then slow down near the end as their efforts near resolution. Still others take detours and then move to solve the problem. I accept the unique pace of each situation and each client. The timing and rate of change is part and parcel of client wisdom. I synchronize my watch to theirs and match my pace to their own.

10. Make no attempt to fix what is already working in the client's life. Do just the opposite: ask the client to do more of what is already working. In this therapy, the client sets the goal, and it is the therapist's job to help the client stay focused on that goal. Doing so means focusing on what is already in motion in the client's life that will support the achievement of that goal. If something is not working for a client in relation to the therapy goal, I ask the client to explore what has worked—even if it has worked only a little bit. If other problems emerge, success is achieved with the stated goal first, and then a contract for other goals is established.

11. Complicated problems do not necessarily call for complicated answers. My experience has been that difficult problems often have unexpected answers—and that the answers are often simpler than the original problem. I have long since discarded the belief that I know (or should know) the answer for every client—and I still believe that each client will discover the next step and the ultimate solution. Letting go of my investment in any particular outcome for the client frees the therapy to go at its own pace and in its own way. The less I control, the more opportunities clients have to make something happen to get the problem solved. When clients do the bulk of the work, the work is sure to get done.

12. Every problem has a pattern, and every pattern includes an exception to its own rule. Look for the exceptions: they are often signposts on the path to the solution. Each problem has a natural ebb and flow, a variation in its severity or in the relative emphasis of its individual elements. This is so because every problem is lodged in a context of feelings, thoughts, and behaviors; as each of these varies from time to time, the problem varies with them. I ask clients to recall those times when they noted a change in the problem or when they were able to affect it in some way. Often the client reaches an unexpected answer. The process of the search itself is one that highlights and reinforces client competence.

13. Thinking, feeling, and behaving differently are part of the process of change; relationships change as individuals change. The context for any problem consists of thoughts, feelings, and behaviors, nested in a matrix of relationships. This context is necessarily different from one that will support the solution to the problem, and the difference between the two contexts must lie in at least one of the three areas. A change in at least one of these areas often leads to a change in the other two—and therefore to a change in the problem. A change in one person inevitably leads to reciprocal changes in the relationships that involve that person.

14. Patterns of problems and solutions occur in time and space; making a change in these dimensions frequently prompts a solution to a problem. Clients are often surprised by how rapidly a situation can change as a result of making a small adjustment in its timing or surroundings. Somehow a problem that is so troubling in one setting or at a given time finds a new meaning when one or both of these elements are changed. Clients report that making these kinds of changes helps them feel more in control of their circumstances, and that feeling may be an important factor in making needed changes. Clients may also spontaneously change the when or where of a problem situation and stumble on a solution for themselves. I encourage any such change proposed by clients.

Here is a summary of the solution-focused approach:

1. Therapy is a setting where clients feel safe and their opinions are honored.

2. As clients set their goals and work toward them, their strengths are identified and highlighted.

3. Change is anticipated, talked about, watched for, and expected.

4. The client charts the course and the therapist gets on aboard as an assistant in that endeavor.

In practicing Solution-Focused Therapy, I view my role as distinguished by these characteristics:

1. I examine my own notions about what the client ought to be doing and set those aside, in favor of the client's choices.

2. My job is to help the client to clarify those choices.

3. My expectation is that each client has made and will make the best possible choices, given the light that he or she has at any given time.

4. I free myself and the therapy from proceeding at a particular pace and in my chosen way; rather, I eagerly watch and learn from the client's pace.

The most basic principle of both lists is that *clients are in charge.* They take the helm of their own ships, select the map and the speed, and choose the destination. My task is to ask good questions and watch for evidence of their competence as they maneuver. That evidence appears as a sign of the power that all human beings have to change or cope with their situations. As the voyage continues, I find that they weather tidal waves and easy currents with equal skill.

And I find that we therapists do too.

3

There Am I:
The Client's View

Think for yourself and let others enjoy the privilege of doing so too.

Voltaire

One can lose everything, but no one is likely to give up an opinion
without a fight.

When clients invite us into their private worlds, what we do there is absolutely crucial. How we behave will determine how long we will be allowed to stay. Our behavior is always under scrutiny by the client, from the initial phone call to the last session.

Honoring what we find in our clients' private worlds and respecting what the therapist and client discover there together means more than doing "no harm." It means being careful not to litter that private world with our own castoff ideas or personal issues. It means taking off the lenses through which we see our own worlds and borrowing our clients' lenses for the purpose of studying their worlds.

The client's path is not our path, and we cannot expect to walk it in the same way that we travel through our own lives. We must be able to look and listen and move there with a special attention to their views. I know from walking my own path that this is what I would want any therapist to do for me. I can do no less for any client who comes to me.

In Solution-Focused Therapy, there is a formula for a written intervention for every client in every session. It is composed of three parts: the client view, client compliments, and the homework task. The first step in developing an intervention is to identify what clients think about their problem and how they view themselves in relation to it. For simplicity's sake, I call these elements the "client view."

The client view includes the client's description of the problem, the client's feelings and emotional expressions, and the client's thoughts and behaviors in relation to the problem. Even if these appear misguided, it helps to accept them as they arise in each session. The emotions that accompany sadness or depression are taken as expected parts of the therapy process; behaviors and thoughts that accompany human dilemmas are accepted as natural and necessary to the healing process.

To do this, I let go of any notion that I know more about my clients' lives than they do. I give up any assumptions that I may have because of my training or work with similar cases, and I let go of any investment in how the therapy should go. I let the client be the expert and rely heavily on what I call "client wisdom."

At its simplest, client wisdom is our clients' ability to make needed changes in steps that make sense to them. Our clients' view of themselves and their problems are powerful tools; within them, they contain the resources that clients need to solve their problems. When we accept these as they are presented, we send our clients a clear message that they are capable. In effect, we are saying, "You *do* know more about your situation than I do. Teach me what it is like for you."

Feelings and emotional expressions are part of client wisdom, part of their healing path. Thoughts and behaviors are parts of this path as well, with each step an approximation to the desired solution.

The first purpose of discerning clients' view of themselves and the problem at hand is to insure cooperation throughout the therapy. This cooperation is the first step on the path that clients take to make their own adjustments. It is the basis on which all change will occur.

Seeing the elements of the client view as client wisdom means trusting clients to know their own paths and letting each of them lead. If the therapist insists on her or his own agenda, resistance is the usual and likely outcome. If the client leads the way, resistance is minimized or disappears altogether.

Because the client view changes from one session to the next, as success toward the goal is realized, it is crucial to keep track of this view in relation to the goal of therapy. The steps for accessing the client view are outlined in the sections that follow.

Accessing the Client View

First, it is useful to note that no new skills are really needed to obtain the client view; all that is needed is the basic counseling skill of paying close attention to what clients say and how they say it. In the course of taking notes during each session, the therapist simply makes a practice of listening for and making a short list of at least three or four phrases that stand out among the many phrases that the client uses in the course of the session. (If there is more than one client in the room, a separate list must be developed for each client present in the session.)

Phrase 1

Phrase 4   *Phrase 2*

Phrase 3

Fig. 3.1. Identifying phrases that carry an emotional charge

With practice, the process of collecting these phrases becomes a habit. The therapist listens for vocal tone and word selection and watches for emotional presentation and body language, as each of these helps to identify the phrases that carry an emotional charge and the descriptions that are most significant to the client. The phrases and descriptions that the therapist selects are illustrated by figure 3.1.

The therapist should select the most emotionally charged phrase in the client's description as the first phrase and rank the remaining phrases as second, third, and fourth, based on the therapist's assessment of the feeling behind the client's descriptions. Each phrase can be as short as one or two words or may be a longer string of words. Ranking the phrases enables the therapist to keep track of what is most important to the client and will help to assure that the client feels heard when these phrases are used later in the intervention.

I like to think of these four phrases forming what looks like a window. This window allows the therapist to see what the clients see about themselves, their problems, and the world in which they live. If the therapist refuses to judge what he or she sees, the client is likely to invite the therapist for a closer look. If the therapist respects the importance of the client's view, the client will invite the therapist to stay even longer, until the job is done.

Case Notes

Zona. *A thirteen-year-old client came to the clinic for her problems at school and at home. She refused to attend school or arrived late and did nothing at home except lie around and listen to loud music. In the course of telling her story, she gave obvious clues about her view of the world, the problem at hand, and herself.*

> *Zona (plopping down in a chair with a huge sigh and a look of disgust):* There is nothing you all can do to help me! I'm just obsessed with the New Kids on the Block!

> *Therapist:* Since there is nothing that we can do to help, what are you doing here?

> *Zona:* Well, it wasn't my idea! Hmmph! My mother says that there is something wrong with me, and all I know is that I am in love with Donnie and the New Kids on the Block. Nothing can help me! Ooh, I am obsessed! *(She lets out a shrill squeal of delight)*

> *Therapist:* What does your mother hope will happen for you here with a counselor?

> *Zona (imitating her mother and pointing her finger):* My mother has lost all hope for my grades, or so she says. She thinks that counseling will help me change. *(Sighing in a romantic way)* I am so obsessed with him. . . .

> *Therapist:* What do you hope will happen to you here?

> *Zona (yawning):* I guess we could get Mom off my back.

Both verbal and nonverbal cues indicated the phrases that held more of her emotion (figure 3.2). The importance to her of these phrases was signalled by her voice and her body language: her tone of voice deepened and grew much louder in the course of saying these phrases, and she accompanied her words by rolling her eyes and throwing up her hands.

In order to enter her world, we simply accepted her view of things as she presented them. We used her language. Our refusal to argue with any of her ideas as-

Phrase 1. "Nothing can help me."

Phrase 4. "There is nothing you all can do to help me."

Phrase 2. "My mother lost all hope for my grades."

Phrase 3. "I am just obsessed."

Fig. 3.2. Zona's phrases

sured two things: she paid attention to what went on in the session and she gave her cooperation to the process of counseling.

Dora. *A 65-year-old woman complained repeatedly about depression that had affected her for twelve years. (She had been diagnosed as having an addiction to prescribed medications and being severely depressed.) She presented the problems she faced in a near whisper. With close attention to her words, I could still find the phrases that were most important to her.*

> *Dora (shaking her head, looking down at her feet, and whispering):* There is no way anyone can help me. It is hopeless.
>
> *Therapist:* What is hopeless?
>
> *Dora:* My situation, of course. Aren't you listening? *(Her voice quickens with an angry tone)*
>
> *Therapist:* What about your situation is hopeless?
>
> *Dora (looking disgusted):* Everything. *(With tears and a strained voice)* My doctors are crackpots, they don't understand me. They don't listen, and ooh—no one can help me.
>
> *Therapist:* What would you like to happen?
>
> *Dora:* I need more drugs of a different kind, and I *(emphatically)* just can't get them to look at what I need. They are too busy.
>
> *Therapist:* What kind of drugs do you think you need?
>
> *Dora:* I don't know. *(Angrily)* Aren't they supposed to know that and tell me? *(Whining)* Oh, there's nothing I can do now.

Again, I selected only four of many possible phrases that this client had used (figure 3.3). That these appeared to be the most potent for her was evidenced by her tone of voice, which became soft and whisperlike, and her body language, which

Phrase 1. "My situation is hopeless."

Phrase 4. "Need more drugs of a different kind."

Phrase 2. "There is no way anyone can help me."

Phrase 3. "My doctors are crackpots."

Fig. 3.3. Dora's phrases

included sitting forward in her chair, pointing her finger in a menacing way, and moaning as she offered these descriptions.

I stayed with her view and made no attempt to challenge any of her ideas or to talk her into any other view. The result was that she was curious about my interest in her, paid close attention to what went on in our session, and allowed me to see more of her world. Over time, she was able to set achievable goals for her therapy and eventually to discover that she had reached them.

Using the Client View

As the therapist collects phrases that are emotionally charged for the client, the picture of the client's world grows larger. This picture is useful for both the client and the therapist as they view it together. The therapist refers to the client's descriptions and uses his or her exact words as they talk about the problem. Clients feel that they are being heard when a therapist accepts their language as well as the content of what they have to say about their problems. When a therapist accepts the view that clients have of themselves, this combination promotes cooperation. Both client and therapist are listening well and offering respect, one to the other.

Note that in addition to accepting the client view of the problem, it is equally important to accept the client view of self. It is not necessary to persuade clients to change how they view themselves in order to set a goal or move toward it. Clients do not need higher self-esteem or self-confidence in order to try a new approach or make a change in their lives. Trying a new approach is usually what raises self-esteem. Clients naturally arrive at an improved sense of self as they solve their problems in a context that honors who they are and what they can do.

Further, as the basis for continued cooperation, the client view is the foundation and first step for writing an intervention, following the three-part formula used in all sessions:

Intervention = Client view + client compliments + homework task

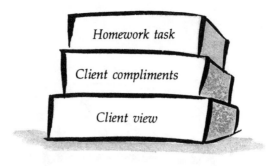

Fig. 3.4. The client view provides a supporting foundation for the other two elements in the formula.

In practice, the second two elements of the formula are meaningless without the influence of the client view. Numerous clients have taught me that they do not hear praise or do homework tasks when I have not understood their views. I must get their views of the problem and themselves first, or I cannot successfully proceed.

I have found it particularly useful to think that I am going to visit in someone else's world for one hour; to the best of my ability, I must behave properly in that world. I ask them to rearrange nothing to make me more comfortable. I work to accept their ideas about their world without judgment, and, out of respect, I choose to speak their language.

Clients feel respected and honored if they are not required to use the language of the therapist—and it is fitting for the therapist to be the more flexible of the two. Clients should not be required to make a mental shift in their own portrayal of their problems in order to help the therapist understand them or feel more comfortable in the therapy.

Further, it is easier for clients to do the real work of changing when they are not distracted by the therapist's need to use different words. Moreover, a therapist's language is often full of professional terms or jargon that clients do not normally understand or use. The usual result when such words are used is that clients feel intimidated and put off by the way the therapist talks.

Most of all, I have discovered that clients really feel they have company in their distress when I use their words. Simply put, they think, "She got it."

At the end of the hour, I can return to my own world; I know from the beginning that I do not have to remain in anyone else's world or continue to use their language if it does not fit my world.

New and old therapists alike must decide whose view is most important. If the client view is most important, then the therapist must identify and set aside his or her own preconceptions. We become visitors in a different world each time we do a therapy session.

Case Note

Corrine. *A thirty-year-old woman presented the problem of never having felt that she fit in. As a recovering person myself, I felt that she was "in my ballpark," a place I knew well. I thought that I knew what she was going to say before she said a single word about her situation. I also felt that I would be very comfortable working with her "since I knew so much about the topic." In short, I entered the room biased against her.*

She could not tell her story to alert and curious ears. Instead, she found someone who had concluded that her story had already been heard. In the course of therapy, she taught me that my life was not her life. She deserved better than what I gave her. Here is a piece of that interview:

> *Corrine:* I don't think I will ever fit anywhere. People just don't seem to like me.
>
> *Therapist:* I know what you mean because I have felt that before many times.
>
> *Corrine:* I just can't feel good about not fitting in.
>
> *Therapist:* It was very hard for me too, but I think I finally got somewhere.

We have drifted from her concerns to my world in two short sentences. I only think I am in her world. Her body language during this part of the interview showed that I was losing her. She looked away from me, looked at her watch while I was talking about myself, and sighed heavily. She could easily be seen as asking herself, "Whose session is this, anyway?"

Instead of dragging us into my world, I could easily have done the same interview with very different responses:

> *Corrine:* I don't think I will ever fit anywhere. People just don't seem to like me.
>
> *Therapist:* What does it mean to you to think that you will never fit anywhere? (*Staying with client, asking her to teach me how it is for her instead of assuming that I know, and using her words.*)
>
> *Corrine:* I just can't feel good about not fitting in.
>
> *Therapist:* If you can't feel good about not fitting in, what needs to happen for you? (*Staying with the client by using her words and asking her to set her own goal.*)

Staying in the Client's World

It is common and natural for therapists to be distracted by familiar words, phrases, and descriptions. It just happens. The effect on therapy can be disastrous. Sessions can just meander meaninglessly, with no clear direction or goal. At any time, a new or veteran therapist can be distracted. The key is to remain curious, to hold the client in high esteem no matter what their status in life, to approach all clients as one would want to be approached, and to stay focused on the therapy goal.

When I have been distracted from the client's world, it is usually by material that I find fascinating. I want more information to feed my fascination, and that is a very different aim than staying with the client's goal for therapy.

Since taking notes during a session helps keep the focus on client material, I deal with my distraction by making a note about the material that caught my attention. Later, on my own time, I look back to see what issue prompted me to reenter my own world and leave the world that the client wants me to know. If the issue that led me astray is personal and unresolved, I find a place that is outside the therapy hour to work on it. I talk to a therapist, trusted friends, or carry it to a support group.

I can usually catch myself now when I am about to steer the session in a direction that I find "interesting." I remind myself through silent self-talk that my focus needs to be on my client. This "self-talk" goes like this: "Whose issue is this? If it's mine, then I can settle it later. What is really important to this client right now?" Any of these responses helps me to return to the focus I want to have in the session and to get back on track with the client.

After all, an hour of therapy is not a long-term visit, and what we do with it is held to a different standard than the polite desire not to offend that a guest and host show to each other. What happens between two people in a therapy setting is much more than doing no harm; honor and respect are required, because they are needed to create a place where clients feel nurtured and know intuitively that they are safe to explore new moves and to do the work they came to do.

Therapists know when they have behaved in a respectful manner, because the client looks forward to and is highly invested in what is going on in the room. Our job is to wait and match the client's pace. We can release any anxiety we have by telling ourselves again that the answer to the client's dilemma is within. We can learn to trust that process to unfold as it needs to unfold.

Accepting the Client's Emotions and Thoughts

Often clients need time to tell their stories, and it is important to move at a pace that matches their own. To do this, I match their vocal tone and rate of speech whenever it is possible to do so (taking care to avoid sounding like I am parroting or mimicking the client). Clients' stories are often heart-wrenching to them; sometimes they are told through a veil of tears, or accompanied by a burst of anger, or muffled by a blanket of depression. If the client's view of the situation is understood, then any emotional response to it or collection of thoughts about it is understandable. If I move myself into a position to see the situation the way the client sees it, then the client's responses will make sense.

Case Notes

Two examples of accepting client emotional expressions follow. Both involve women of about age thirty who had come for therapy.

Cindy. *In the first case, the client looked a bit disheveled and distracted. In the first fifteen minutes of her session, she began to cry. Her crying then turned to wailing. She wailed for nearly fifteen minutes. The sound was disturbing and deafening. I knew that she could be heard by others in the building.*

It occurred to me that I had no right to interrupt this painful process. I also thought, "This needs to happen." I leaned forward and whispered to her, "That's right, do it till you don't need to do it anymore." She responded by wailing louder than before.

Her wailing went on for a few more minutes, and then she stopped herself. What was hurting her so badly? She talked of the relationship she had tried so fiercely to have with her own mother. We looked at what she had tried to do and the lack of success she had experienced.

Spontaneously, she told me that she could see herself as a little girl. The image she saw was of a tiny girl, alone and crying, cold and hungry. We talked for a while about that image:

Therapist: What does the little girl want?

Cindy: She is cold and hungry.

Therapist: What needs to happen for her?

Cindy: Someone needs to take care of her. No one did.

Therapist: Yes. What do you think she might need?

Cindy: I have to talk some more to her.

Her conversation went back to her mother's brutality and how her attempts to be what her mother wanted had all failed. I asked if it were possible for her to please her mother. She stated that she thought it might be impossible.

Therapist: If it is impossible, what needs to happen?

Cindy: Someone has to take care of me, because she didn't.

She began to wail again, and it seemed that years of pain were being dumped out on the carpet between us. There was the sense of deep disappointment in her—a sense that she had never been parented. The wailing seemed an appropriate response, even now, years later, to the intensity of this pain. I felt glad that I was there, so that she would not have to take this terrifying walk alone. She had certainly been alone the first time she had taken it, and I was privileged to accompany her the second time around. A few minutes later, her wailing stopped.

Therapist: Was there ever a time that you found you were taking good care of yourself?

Cindy: I'm not sure. I'll have to think on that.

I made an appointment with her for the next day. When she arrived, she looked different. Her hair was combed, her dress was neat, and her mood also seemed changed.

Cindy: I want to tell you what I did for the little girl last night. I asked what she liked to eat and she told me. I took her out to get the kind of food she likes, and then we went to look in the stores. I went alone, but I was with her.

Therapist: How did that help?

Cindy: Well, she knows that someone loves her and that someone is me. I liked being with her. I think she feels better today, and so do I.

Therapist: You do, don't you?

Cindy (smiling): Yes.

Therapist: How do you explain that you and she are feeling better?

Cindy: I noticed her and got her something she wanted. You want to know what else I did?

Therapist: Of course.

Cindy: I skipped the morning sessions of the conference, even when my friends wanted me to go with them, and I took her out shopping instead. I got her some things that she likes. Found some things that she likes that I didn't know about.

Therapist: How did that help?

Cindy: I think I have to take care of her and me. Now I know this.

What spontaneously followed after the outward display of emotion was her discussion of the needs of her "inner child." She not only discussed these needs, but also began to meet some of them and reflect on the experience. She picked the time and the methods that worked for her. If I had chosen to assign these activities to her, the outcome and the response would have been much different. She discovered her own wisdom, led by her own feelings, thoughts, and behaviors.

Bear in mind that Cindy had never heard of "inner child" work. All she knew was that there was a little girl inside of her, desperate for nurturing. Her wisdom led her to this little girl and to the right things to do for her.

Margo. In the second case, the client came to discuss a matter that she had not worked on before. Apparently, she had been sexually abused at an early age and now wanted to explore this issue for the first time. We spent the first five minutes of the session reviewing the topic in a general way, and she appeared to have no trouble with our discussion. But when we turned to specifics, she suddenly blurted out, "I have to throw up."

She seemed ashamed, embarrassed, and resolved to vomit all at the same time. I picked up a nearby trash can and held it out to her. I said, "That's right. I'll hold this for you. Do it until you think you are finished."

She responded right away by throwing up. I held the can. In doing so, and thinking about what was going on and my role in it, I experienced a wash of joy over my entire being. I wasn't sure what she was experiencing on the inside or what kind of agony she was revisiting, but I knew that I had to be there with her. It was not a chore to hold the can; the action of vomiting held her agony, and holding this receptacle meant that I would help her release that agony. I found the will to trust her body's needs and took my direction from those needs. It was a privilege to do so—the sheer privilege of honoring the wisdom of her physical nature. I made no attempt to address her feelings, much less to shame or redirect them into some other outlet. I accepted their part in the wisdom of the moment.

As suddenly as she had begun vomiting, she stopped. When she had recovered, I asked her to tell me what this meant to her. She replied that she did not know. What, then, did she need to do for herself in order to work on the issue of sexual abuse?

Margo: I need to understand what is happening to me. I feel so guilty, and then I throw up.

Therapist: What do you make of this? What meaning do you give it?

Margo: I think it means that I am very guilty about all that happened and maybe there's something wrong with that.

Therapist: What do you think you want to do about that?

Margo: I don't want to feel guilty anymore.

Therapist: What would you be feeling if you weren't feeling guilty?

Margo: Feeling lighter, I'd be feeling lighter. There's a black cloud over me now. I feel very heavy.

Therapist: What do the black cloud and the heaviness mean to you?

Margo: It means that I have to do something now to help myself.

Therapist: What do you think that is?

Margo: I've got to feel less guilty.

Therapist: Are there times when you do feel less guilty?

Margo: I think about this stuff a lot, and that's when I feel heavy. I don't know about times when I don't feel so guilty.

Therapist: When was a time that you did something or thought something or felt something besides guilt?

Margo: When I am doing things I want to do or thinking about what I want. I think I might feel better then, but I am not sure. I think something has to come out of me. I have to get rid of something inside me.

We talked about the changes she wanted to make in her life and what she had thought about doing to begin those changes. She said that she would take a weekly bus trip to a nearby city for regular therapy to deal with the guilt. I was amazed at the degree of her commitment to her own healing. She asked about the traits of a good counselor and handed me a pen to write them down for her. She asked about books to read on sexual abuse and recovery from it. We listed those. She signaled the end of our time together by saying, "I am ready to get on with this." As I finished writing down the list of traits and book titles that she had asked for, she said, "I'd like you to keep my pen."

I felt that this exchange completed a circuit of healing for her. She had a need to give something, however small, because she had begun to receive in a healthy way.

In both cases, these sessions were extraordinary expressions of emotions that could not have been communicated so vividly in any other way. By trusting what happened as client wisdom, as steps in a path that only they could outline, I was able to leave each of them free in the apparent safety of an honoring atmosphere to move herself forward on a healing path. Each step was theirs to make and mine to follow. The questions I asked were needed simply to make sure that I understood the meanings they attached to what was happening to them, the things that had helped them before, and the next step on the path.

Questions like these move the therapy toward the goal of resolution. This agenda should not take priority over clients' need to tell their stories, and emotional responses on their part need to be honored. I do not attempt to change what the client is doing in the room; rather, I assume that the emotions are a healthy part of normal expression around troublesome issues. The emotions, along with thoughts and behaviors, are part of the makeup of each client's wisdom.

Short of clients injuring themselves in front of me, I allow them the freedom to move about and express themselves as they need to do. This again is part of a nurturing atmosphere. It takes time and practice for therapists to find a point of balance between listening to the client story and finding a place for questions that move the therapy forward.

In practice, moving forward means taking our understanding of the client view on to the next step: setting a stated goal for the therapy.

4

Setting a Goal for Therapy

For therapy to fail, refuse to set a goal.

Jay Haley

It is difficult, if not impossible, to know you have arrived, if you didn't figure out where you were headed in the first place.

Since Solution-Focused Therapy is goal oriented, the first session is used to formulate and set a specific goal. The client selects the goal and sets the priority. Even though the client may come to therapy with several goals or go on to discover additional goals in later sessions, I have found it most effective to begin with one goal, contract for it, meet success with it, and then contract for other goals.

The premise behind this approach is that therapy must be directed by the client's chosen goal. This goal is tracked throughout the course of therapy, and everything that is done in the sessions is done in relation to it. In part, this approach is valuable because it keeps the therapy on course, sets time limits for it, and helps make it cost efficient. More significantly, setting a goal means that the success of the therapy will be clear and duly noted by the participants. If additional goals are needed, they can then be negotiated; if not, the therapy ends at a point obvious to client and therapist alike.

When clients tell me what appear to be unrelated stories, my response is to ask how this particular event is related to their goal. I find that the new material often is related, even though the connection is not obvious to the client or the therapist. Each different story told in any particular therapy session is often a variation on a theme that is related to the goal itself. If the therapist asks, "How is this related to the goal you have chosen?" then the client has to work on helping the therapist understand the connection.

In my estimation, it is perfectly fine for clients to bring in something new each week; my role in this is simply to insist that clients connect the material they bring to the therapy goal. I ask that the client think about that question and help me to understand how the events in their lives are related. If the events are connected to the goal, then the problem may be a complex one, and we are doing well to reveal more of its aspects, even though this may happen session after session. If the new material is not connected, then the client and I both agree that it is not. My response then is usually to ask the client to set priorities and recontract for these goals later.

This same approach is also effective with clients who have multiple goals or come to therapy with a litany of lifelong complaints. The client begins by identifying a specific goal and starts to work on that; additional goals can be negotiated as success is attained with the goal the client has given the first priority.

Nature of the Goal

The problem that a client brings to therapy may be oriented toward behavior, thoughts, or feelings, and clients usually present problems predominantly in one of these ways. Their conversation about the problem at hand is full of words that are feeling oriented, such as "I *feel* badly when my son leaves home without telling me." A client presenting a problem in a cognitive manner might say "I *think* that our marriage is all over," while the partner, behavioral in orientation, might say "What can I *do* to make this marriage work?" Accordingly, as I begin to understand the client view and respond to it in client language, I ask the client to set a working goal that is either feeling oriented, thinking or cognitive oriented, or behavioral in nature, as determined by the way that he or she presented the problem.

In Solution-Focused Therapy, questions are used as interventions throughout the sessions; this process begins with the first session when the goal questions are asked. Since goals differ for voluntary and involuntary clients, different questions are asked in order to help these different clients set goals.

Voluntary clients are ususaly more responsive to the task of choosing goals and more motivated to work toward attaining the goals they have set. Involuntary clients begin therapy as the result of a decision that someone else has made for them, and these clients often see the goal which that decision imposes on them as a mistaken one. Over time, as their sessions continue, the experience of having their viewpoint honored helps make involuntary clients more willing to set goals and work toward achieving them. These goals are often the same ones specified by the person who referred the client. Although the initial questions for the two types of client differ, the strategies for setting goals with either type of client actually vary only slightly.

Setting a Goal for a Voluntary Client

A voluntary client is one who appears for therapy on her or his own and is usually highly motivated to work on issues. Normally the interview begins with polite exchanges of general conversation. The therapist then asks any one of these questions:

- What brings you here today?

- How can I help you?

- What is it that absolutely has to change?

- How will you know that therapy was a success for you? What will be different for you?

- How will you know that I have been helpful to you? What will be different for you?

- What will be going on in your life when you have finished therapy that will let you know that therapy was a good idea?

These questions can be somewhat startling for clients, especially if they are familiar with other kinds of therapies. The usual responses include such answers as "I will feel less depressed" or "I will feel better" or "My self-confidence will improve"— vague, general answers that do not specify a goal. The first therapy task, then, is to help clients to become more specific about goals. This is done by accepting their initial responses and then asking questions like these:

- And when you are feeling better, what will be different? What will you be feeling instead? What will have happened that contributed to the new feeling?

- When you are less depressed, what will you notice is different for you? What will you be feeling instead *(feeling)*? What will you be thinking instead *(cognitive)*? What will you be doing instead *(behavioral)*?

- When you are more self-confident, what will be going on then for you?

For clients with a "feeling" orientation, I use a "feeling" question to help them set their goals. I then follow the goal-setting question with another "feeling" question, such as: "What will be a clear indication that you are feeling better?"

If the client presents his or her question with a cognitive orientation, I ask this question: "When your situation is better, what will you be thinking differently?" I follow that question with a version of this question: "What kinds of thoughts will you be thinking that you are not thinking now?"

If the client has a behavioral orientation, I ask this question: "When the problem is solved, what will you be doing differently?" and follow with a question such as: "What kinds of things will be you be doing that you are not doing now?"

Case Notes

Setting a feeling-oriented goal. *A thirteen-year-old female client informed our staff that she "felt" very bad about herself and that she believed "nothing could help her." She told us that she just wanted to feel better about herself. Here is part of that discussion:*

Therapist: So, you want to feel better about yourself?

Mia: Yes, I feel terrible, I can't do anything right and I feel like everybody is laughing at me.

Therapist: When you are feeling better about yourself, what kind of feeling will you have?

Mia: I will like myself the way I am. What other people think about me won't make any difference.

Therapist: What kind of feeling will that be?

Mia: I will feel good. A good feeling.

Therapist: What do you think it will take for you to feel good like that?

Mia: I may have to give up feeling bad. I don't know if I can do that. I feel bad all the time.

The good news is that Mia does not have to know the answers to any of these questions at the moment they are asked, and her answers can even be as fuzzy as they are here. The questions are *interventions* aimed in the direction she wants to go, and they ask her to think about what she wants and to narrow that focus to an achievable goal. For the moment, her achievable goal is to "give up feeling bad."

Setting a thought-oriented goal. *Terri came to our clinic with an absorbing attention on her past. She could not stop thinking about the loss of a dear friendship. She told us that* *she thought of the lost friend about 95 percent of the time. It was fairly easy to help her identify a goal. Here is some of that interview:*

> *Terri:* Yes, I think about how this woman quit being my friend—just started doing things she knew would hurt me, like dating the guy I want to date. *(She begins to cry)*

> *Therapist:* How much of the time do you think about this?

> *Terri (still crying):* All the time, wouldn't you? I mean she was my very best friend. I can't believe it.

> *Therapist:* What percentage of the time would you say you think about this friend?

> *Terri (answering through her tears):* About 95 percent of the time.

> *Therapist:* Is that too much for you?

> *Terri (looking up and sounding a bit stunned):* Well, I guess so. I can't get anything done, because I can't stop thinking about her. It's driving me crazy.

> *Therapist:* What would you like to do about this?

> *Terri:* Not think about her so much, and I don't want to hurt anymore over this.

> *Therapist:* What percentage of the time would you say you could live with in regards to thinking about her?

> *Terri:* Maybe only 15 percent of the time.

> *Therapist:* When you are no longer thinking about her, what do you think you will be thinking about instead?

> *Terri:* I'll be thinking about what interests me.

The goal here is very clear; it is even quantified, which is helpful. The goal is to "not think so much about her anymore" and therefore stop hurting. The interview helped Terri focus on a clear goal, and her goal in turn directed the therapy toward an examination of her thoughts and the changes she wants to make in them. Accordingly, the last question in the interview begins this process by asking her to think about what she will do to counteract her current thought process.

Setting a behavioral goal. *Jim referred himself for therapy to work on getting along better with his wife of five years. She did not come to therapy, but he was clear about wanting to make changes in the ways he approached her.*

> *Therapist:* So, Jim, what has to be different for you so that you know therapy was a good idea?

> *Jim:* I have to get along better with my wife. She says a lot of it's my fault, and maybe she's right. I could do better.

> *Therapist:* What happens between the two of you that lets you know that something needs to be different on your side?

> *Jim:* Well, I yell and scream a lot, especially if I am tired—but she nags, God is she good at that!

> *Therapist:* So, is it your yelling and screaming that has to change?

Jim: I think so. I never thought it was a problem. And it still doesn't strike me as so bad, she just thinks it is. And she's right about other things, so maybe she's right about this.

Therapist: What do you think you need to do to change your yelling and screaming?

Jim: I need to cut down on it or not raise my voice. I think my loud voice really scares my wife—'cause she grew up in a crazy family.

Therapist: When you are not raising your voice what do you think you will be doing instead?

Jim: I will hold what I think more.

Jim was pretty clear about what he needed to do, and, although not completely convinced, he was able to identify some needed changes in his behavior. His immediate goal is to cut down on the number of times he yells or to lower his voice and hold back some on his reactions.

In all three cases, the goals have some things in common. They are all measurable, countable, and repeatable. In Solution-Focused Therapy, a good goal is one that is easily tracked—first, by the client, and second, by the therapist. A goal for therapy that is easy to achieve is one that is clear, specific, and achievable.

Typical Responses of Voluntary Clients

Voluntary clients are often eager to solve their problems (or have the therapist solve their problems for them). They are willing to work (or appear willing) and yet find it difficult to set a specific goal. For one thing, few clients expect such a direct approach. More often, they expect much history taking and discussion of why something in their past occurred. In Solution-Focused Therapy, "why" sets up an insoluble riddle. We are more interested in achieving the goal set by the client.

In response to any type of goal question, clients are likely to respond by saying "I don't know" or "I'm not sure" or to answer in other vague terms. Typical examples are "I want to feel better" or "I want to have a better self-concept" or " I want to do better." Most often I hear this kind of response to the question about what will be different: "I won't be _____ anymore." Prompted to set a goal, clients tell us what they will *not* be doing, thinking, or feeling.

The untrained therapist's ear will hear these common client responses as "resistance" or simply let them bring an end to that part of the discussion. Beginning therapists often drop the whole question of goals right here. They look puzzled and often comment on how "uncooperative" their client is. While it may appear that responses like these are confusing and frustrating, a few fairly simple strategies are available to move the therapy forward.

Unknown goals. For clients who do not know what their goals are, a straightforward request from the therapist can be just the thing to move toward a clear goal. Some good responses are:

- If you were sure, what do you think would be different for you?

- If you did know, what would you want to be different?

- Since you really don't know, let's say that your problem is solved. What changed? What are you doing (*or thinking or feeling*) differently?

Finally, this one helps some clients "see" how the problem will look once it is solved:

- Picture yourself on a movie screen. You no longer have this problem. What are you doing (*or thinking or feeling*) instead?

These same questions can also be used with feeling-oriented or thought-oriented goals.

Vague goals. For those with vague goals, it is a good idea to leave their reasons for being vague out of the discussion if you can. If a client wants to "feel better," I often ask this question: "And, when you are feeling better, what will you be feeling then?" For those who are thought oriented, I ask: "When you have a better self-concept, what will you be thinking that is different than now?" For the doers, I ask: "When you are doing better, what is it that you will be doing that you are not doing now?"

The word "instead" is an important word for most clients and especially for those clients who answer with negative goals. I simply ask: "When you are no longer doing (*or thinking or feeling*) what you are doing now, what will you be doing instead?" This word is a powerful addition to the therapist's skills. "Instead" nails down an objective, a real or possible goal. Moreover, making sure that a goal is set is the therapist's job and is not necessarily in the mind of the client. A few well-worded questions using the word "instead" will make the difference here.

Occasionally clients will refuse to state a goal or indicate that they are uncomfortable doing so. Either way, I try to honor their approach and match it. For these cases, the therapist can ask this question to move therapy forward: "When the problem (*unspecified*) is solved, what will you be doing (*or thinking or feeling*) that you are not doing now?" Although the goal remains unspecified, this question has the advantage of turning the client's thoughts toward the future and a possible solution for the problem. The goal becomes the positive one of thinking, feeling, or behaving in the new way, rather than the negative one of giving up the old ways. The client can even refuse to disclose the nature of the problem, and it can still be solved. (deShazer 1991)

Multiple goals. Some clients have so many complaints that it is hard for them to narrow their focus. They seem to have and cling to a global understanding of their problems. In session, they list all their complaints, hanging them in front of the therapist like clothes on a clothesline. I approach situations like these this way: "What would you like to work on first?" or "What has to be solved first?" or "What is most important to you to get done first?" These questions ensure the selection of a workable goal.

Often clients will answer these questions with "I don't know." The therapist may feel compelled to push the question, give up, or select the issue that the therapist feels is most important for the client to work on. I resist all these temptations by matching the client's response with my own "I don't know, either." I may acknowledge how hard it can be to choose, but I gently and firmly stay with the question of deciding what has to be solved first. The eventual outcome is that the client either chooses or does not return for the next session. Most often, the client chooses.

Clients who change goals. Clients who change goals during individual sessions and from one session to the next have something in common with those who have long lists of complaints. They want to complain and to have someone hear them, but may not want to change anything. There are folks like this. Steven deShazer once noted that clients like these were looking for a different kind of therapy, one that does not move. Or, he said, "they are looking to hire the therapist as a relative (deShazer 1991)."

For the client who changes goals often, I ask them to connect the new goal to the previously stated goal for therapy. If they can connect the two goals, then that raises the importance of the original goal. If they cannot connect the two for me, then I ask which one needs attention first. The first time this happens, we may decide to change to the second goal—but we stay with and finish that one before contracting for any other goal.

The goal is a crucial step to problem resolution. It is truly difficult to know when you have arrived if you did not know where you were headed in the first place. If everyone involved in the therapy knows where they are headed, that is, the final goal has been named, then all will know when the goal has been reached. Success is more likely.

Setting Goals for Involuntary Clients

These clients find their way to the therapist's door at someone else's insistence or suggestion. It is rarely a decision they agree with. They usually balk at the idea of therapy and remain unmotivated to work with the therapist. Based on their life experience and their view of it, these attitudes make sense to them.

For the hour they are with me, these views make sense to me too. I am a visitor in their worlds, and, as a guest, I behave myself in accordance with their opinions. The questions I ask are chosen to let them know that I respect their views. Here are some examples of questions to use with involuntary clients and some of their usual responses.

Case Notes

"Someone sent me here"

Therapist: Since your mom sent you to me, what will you do differently to make sure you do not have to come back?

Client: Since I don't need to be here, I gotta let my mom know I am doing all right.

Therapist: What do you need to do to let her know that you are doing all right?

In this case, the therapist has accepted the client's stated wish to not be in therapy and asks the client what he has to do to convince another he no longer needs it. In practice, this amounts to making a change in the needed direction. What has been avoided is a repetition of the fight that the client had with the person who referred him, in this case, his mother.

"I don't have a problem"

Client: I don't have a problem. They are wrong about me. I don't drink as much as they think I do.

Therapist: Since they are wrong about you, what will they have to see you doing differently to know that counseling is not for you?

Client: I don't know. You would have to ask them.

Therapist: What do you think they would say if they were here?

Client: They would tell you I need to stop drinking.

Therapist: Are they right?

Client: Maybe I could cut down some. I don't need to stop.

The usual fight or resistance can be over that quickly. Here are some alternative forms of the questions used with this type of involuntary client.

- Since this is someone else's idea, what will you have to do to show that this was a bad idea to send you here?

- What will you have to do to get them off your back?

- Since this is someone else's idea, how do you explain that you are here talking to me?

These questions do two simple things that make life easier for the therapist and move the therapy forward. First, they honor the hostile position that involuntary clients often have. Second, they pose a goal that these clients *do* agree with: the goal of getting the referring person "off their backs." This attitude can be very motivating, and we can use that motivation to help the client set a reasonable goal. The best news is that there is no fight. The hostile person has an ally.

The court-ordered client

Client: Court sent me. I didn't do it.

Therapist: The court thinks you have a problem and you do not agree. What do they need to see you doing that will convince them it is not necessary for you to come here for counseling?

Client: Gotta stay away from Sandy, my wife.

Therapist: When was the last time you found you were able to do that?

A variation of this same approach is: "What do they need to see you doing that will tell them they are wrong about you?" Another version also works: "I'm surprised you showed up, since they are wrong about you. What do you need to do here and now so that this hour is not a waste of your time?"

Questions like these take into account the views of persons who do not want to be in therapy. These clients rarely expect anyone, much less the therapist, to respect their views, and they are often a bit surprised when this happens. Their surprise may be accompanied by confusion. This confusion is helpful, because it blocks their usual attempt to fight the old fight of resistance. When the therapist attempts to see their view, their attention is roused and they often become more cooperative. Tyler's case provides a good example of this process.

Case Note

Tyler. *A Cherokee man was sent to me for therapy. In his first few sentences he let me know that "women were stupid," that "he didn't need a counselor," and that "white women were especially stupid." I accepted these views as being true for him and representative of his experience with whites and in particular with white women. I responded by asking him, since women were stupid and white women were especially stupid, and since he knew that he didn't need a counselor, how did he account for the fact that he made it in to see me? He replied that his wife made him come about his drinking, which really was not a problem anyway.*

Therapist: What was it that made you come in, since you don't have a
      drinking problem?

Tyler: Well, I'm sure that I don't really have one on weekdays anyway.

Therapist: What has to change so that she won't send you to see me anymore?

Tyler: She wants me to stop drinking so much on the weekend.

In the space of just a few short sentences between us, there had been no argument about his views, just a recognition of how he felt and a question about how he
had made it in to see me. From there, we clarified with great ease the exact nature
of his drinking and what had to be changed in his life. Each question matched where
he was and joined him there. There was no fight for power. If anything took the place
of the resistant attitude he usually assumed, it was curiosity. He was curious about a
therapist who would not fight or persuade. This kept his attention. He could not resist
a therapist who refused to hold up her end of the resistance game. At the end of this
session, he was asked by other staff if he would talk to me again, and he answered
yes.

Both lists of questions, for voluntary and involuntary clients, set the therapy in
motion toward a goal the client believes is reasonable. Goal-oriented therapies do just
that. With a goal in mind, this therapy moves to look at past successes, the subject of
the next two chapters.

5

Using Client Strengths

*In recognizing the humanity of our fellow beings, we pay ourselves
the highest tribute.*

Thurgood Marshall

Think a minute. What did you do the last time someone
noticed something you did well and you believed that what
they said was true?

Searching for client strengths is crucial for two reasons. First, and most importantly, client strengths are the source of the solutions in Solution-Focused Therapy; a focus on client strengths is seen as the most direct route to developing an intervention that will work for the client's chosen goal. A second important benefit is that clients seem to listen better if the therapist has not only understood their view of themselves and their situation, but also finds something positive in what they have been doing, no matter how desperate the situation is.

As therapists, we can further both of these objectives by assigning ourselves the simple task of complimenting our clients. To do so, I search diligently for my clients' strengths as they tell their stories. I look for any sign, no matter how minimal it might be, that they have tried to solve their problem. Each effort is noted and honored. These compliments are used at the end of each session as the second part of the intervention.

As I perform this task, I remain aware of the client view and continue to accept it as true for the client. I remember that the client requires a mirroring from the therapist throughout therapy, so I do not move ahead to point out apparent strengths or use words to describe them that my clients would not use. Rather, I operate as if I were standing behind my clients' shoulders and looking in the same direction that they are looking. I still see what they see; the strengths I acknowledge are attributes that have proved useful to them. I let go of any need I have for the strength I see to be of any particular size or shape; my only job is to appreciate what I see, honor it in the same language that the client has used, and remember it by taking note of the useful things the client is doing to solve the problem. I make written notes of any coping mechanism that has helped at all, whether the client is aware of it or not.

Mirroring means accepting what the client brings. A mirror doesn't change its subject; it accepts the shapes and colors before it and offers an exact reflection of the same image back to the subject. In human interaction, mirroring takes on the form of accepting statements such as "I see," "Hmm," "I am sure that you felt that way," or

"Right." The experience for the client is similar to the mirroring that mothers do with their infants: the infant coos, and then the mother coos. The interaction is affirming.

Most importantly, I take note of the strengths that clients view as strengths for themselves. The strengths that become evident as clients tell their stories and respond to the questions I ask are not always apparent to them. But since I expect strengths to emerge, I wait and watch for these and appreciate each to myself when it surfaces. I mark these developments as they appear with short affirmative responses such as "Yes, you did, didn't you?" or "Wow!" or "Really?" or "You did that?" Any such act of appreciation from the therapist is met with client responses that tell more about the use of their strength. They speak with pride. They speak with renewed energy.

Yet because I continue to use their language and to search for their strengths, the experience can be unsettling in some ways. Most clients do not expect this approach from their therapists and are somewhat startled to be questioned about their strengths. They expect advice, corrections, and answers. When I refuse to make the responses they expect, the surprise or even confusion that some clients feel can itself help to keep their attention focused on the goal. Some confusion in the therapy session can be helpful, as the client must search for a new way to respond.

I have also found that appreciating clients for characteristics and actions that they know to be true about themselves gives them hope. While it is certainly not what most clients are expecting to hear, it is more encouraging for them to see themselves finding their own answers. Hope breeds hope, and the entire setting becomes full of expectation for change.

Client Compliments: The Teachable Moment

Compliments follow the client view in the formula for a written intervention. As the therapist notes client strengths, these are recorded; of the many strengths that are noted, some are selected to share with the client at the close of each session. These strengths are presented in the form of compliments that the client can readily accept as true about himself or herself.

Client compliments come directly from the language that clients use to tell their stories; once again, this is done to improve the chance that the client will accept what is being offered and cooperate with the task. Since their own words are not changed, the praise that clients hear is believable, and they recognize without hesitation that they do have this or that ability or trait that the therapist singles out to praise.

I have noticed that when I read or recall the client view and the strengths that clients believe to be true for them, the effect on clients is hypnotic. They become fascinated with the words used to describe them (which are, of course, their own

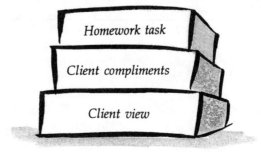

Fig. 5.1. Compliments follow the client view in the formula for a written intervention.

words about themselves). This is what Milton Erickson called a "teachable moment." When clients hear their own language being used to describe their own strengths, they are drawn to the wisdom within. Their listening ability soars and their attention to issues in therapy improves. They are validated and honored. It is a stunning moment. It is often a joyous one, too.

In Solution-Focused Therapy, the teachable moment is that exact time in the session when client attentiveness is most acute. This moment inevitably occurs after clients hear the therapist acknowledge their own views, followed by a set of compliments paid to a list of their strengths. It is at this moment that client interest in what the therapist is saying is at its highest point; it is no coincidence that the words the therapist is saying are the clients' own words and that these words are of utmost importance to them. Hearing their views and strengths draws clients' attention to what is said next. That next piece is the homework task for the client to do in between sessions to further the therapy goals set by the client.

Client Responses to Compliments

Client verbal responses and body language are noticeable when the therapist has performed the task of complimenting well. Often facial muscles relax, and clients become transfixed by the therapist's words; momentarily, they look hypnotized. Their eyes and ears are focused upon the message from the therapist; it is as if they are hearing the wisdom they need for the first time. At the very least, they are being affirmed in a nurturing atmosphere—maybe for the first time.

When their strengths are recalled in their own words, clients often interrupt the reading of the intervention message to tell us how they did what they did or why they are the way they are. I am reminded of the way that children will often respond to a parent's or another adult's praise by saying "And you know what else I do well?"

In part, it is simply a good experience to be caught doing something well. Moreover, it is really a good feeling to be caught doing something well when you are *not* expecting that to happen. When this message comes from someone who accepts your view of your life and takes note of your strengths, it is a nurturing and rewarding experience. Most clients return for more. It is a very pleasant moment for the therapist as well.

In my work, I have noted that the absolute peak of the compliment experience is when clients compliment themselves on their own efforts or improvement. It is one thing to hear a therapist point out strengths or improvements; it is another for clients to recognize and appreciate their own hard work. This recognition brings a deep satisfaction and an increased sense of self-esteem—all self-induced.

There are times when the compliments do not fit. If the therapist has changed the client's words, then a puzzled look may come across the face of the client. Or the therapist may have selected minor good points to praise and missed a glaringly obvious strength. In either case, the puzzled look is the key that either some rephrasing of the compliment or a further explanation from the therapist will be needed as the intervention is read to the client.

Using the Client's Strengths

The formula for the written intervention is again:

Intervention = Client view + client compliments + homework task

The client view has been seen as the basis or foundation of the other two elements. A therapist who acknowledges clients' views gets their attention and keeps it. As clients hear the intervention being read to them, praise for their strengths further hones the attention they pay to the entire therapy message. Hearing both read by the therapist creates a moment of maximum attention. They are ready to hear the task and highly likely to do it.

As a single client or a member of a group or family, any client is waiting to hear what has been done well. This need does not seem to diminish over a number of therapy sessions; rather, if the intervention fits well enough in each of these first two categories, the client will feel honored and held in high regard. The rest of the message will be heard and heeded.

The fit only has to be good enough. Although a "good enough" fit varies from client to client, I usually find that recalling four potent phrases from the client view and presenting three or four compliments to each client assures continued attention to what is being said in the entire message and a good fit.

Seeing Things Upside Down

Just as the therapist may need to make some adjustments in order to accept what clients have to say about themselves and their problems, so too it is often necessary for the therapist to be rather flexible in order to identify client strengths. For my part, I have found it essential to be prepared to challenge my own personal ideas of what kinds of behavior are "strong" or "effective" in order to see things the way my clients see them. Sometime a little flexibility is all that is needed—a slight rephrasing of the definitions I use or a small relaxation of the kind of stances I take in my own life. Other times we need to go a bit further. And often it is necessary to see things upside down.

For instance, no matter what role anger plays in my own personal environment, in the context of a client's world it may be helpful for me to view the anger that a client expresses as "extreme concern" or a "considerable investment in the outcome" of a certain event. Behaviors that could be labelled timidity or slowness to respond or even silence in another context can also be seen as "necessary caution." Talkative or verbose clients can also be described as persons who are "devoted to detail" or "concerned with complete accuracy." Others who worry incessantly can be viewed as persons who "care deeply about their situations to the point of self-sacrifice." Even codependency can be seen as "necessary and devoted attention to the management of one's affairs even to the point of extreme personal sacrifice." Does this sound ridiculous? On one level, as a textbook definition of behavior, it is. And yet if the therapist takes this position with a codependent, that client *will agree and feel heard.* And when there is no argument, then the client can begin to change.

Taking stands like these doesn't just make it easier for me to join clients in their view of the world; more often than not, as soon as I accept where the clients are, they are off to find healthier ways to conduct their business. It's as if hearing me agree with what seems necessary for them to do in their lives frees them to find other ways to behave. In any case, persuasion is not necessary, and the usual fight for control is over. At the very least, there is no argument about what the client is doing, and there is no advice giving that offers the client one more chance to resist what a helping person has to say. In the place of conflict is a sense of peaceful cooperation between client and therapist. And, more often than not, the needed changes begin to occur.

Dora's case was introduced in chapter 3; she was a 65-year-old woman who had been dually diagnosed as having an addiction to prescribed medications and being severely depressed. Here is how I found examples of strength in the way that she presented her problem.

Case Note

Dora. *In the course of telling me her story, Dora noted several strengths that she had. She let me know that she had been "strong at times," although this was "no longer so." She knew that she needed help and was really looking for it. Her situation was very desperate because the doctors at the inpatient unit were real "crackpots."*

In order to honor her view and find strengths within it, I adjusted my internal definitions of strength for her. I offered her these compliments:

> *Therapist:* I am impressed that you could realize that you need help at this time and that you remembered times when you were strong. I commend you on your willingness to seek help and to assess the level of capabilities of those offering you help.

Her initial response was amazement; this was followed by close attention to the rest of the therapy message, including her homework task. Her nonverbal behaviors signaled that the fit was good enough; she appeared mesmerized, her facial muscles relaxed, and she nodded her head. She felt heard. She listened for the intervention and agreed to do the homework task. She would continue to return to therapy until she felt her depression lift.

Again, I was careful to use her words and ideas and to search for strength within her view. I reminded myself that she had the capacity to heal herself at her own particular pace and in her own way. I hoped she would show me how she could do that. Her own wisdom emerged when we looked together for her strength.

In many cases, clients continue to see themselves as weak even while they are clearly solving their problems. At other times, they credit the therapist for any improvement or lack of it. In all these situations, I simply agree with the client's view. In Dora's case, she continued to ask me when she would get better and when I was going to help her. I simply assured her that she was correct to be concerned about when she would get better and what I was going to do to help her.

Case Note

"I want the best!" *In another case, I was asking solution-focused questions and the dialogue with the client was progressing nicely. In the middle of what was apparently going to be a textbook interview, my client began to scream at me:*

> *Client:* You human relations expert! I want the best care for my children, and I am not sure that you are it!

Needless to say, this attitude seemed to come from nowhere. I took a deep breath and replied:

> *Therapist:* I really respect how you are willing to take on anybody, including me, to get proper care for your children. Only a concerned and caring mother would do that.

She readily agreed and continued with the rest of her interview with me. This way of looking at her outburst provided valuable material for the compliments in the final written intervention.

What is clear in these cases is the absolute necessity of letting others have their current views and honoring these views as they come up in the session. Sometimes clients' views of themselves and their situation is literally all that they have left. The therapist can do great damage by taking these away. Or the therapist can offer a great affirmation by joining clients on their own path. It is a choice with staggering consequences.

The search for client strength begins with the client view and is carried on through client compliments. This search is continued by the probe for exceptions, times when the problem somehow got better, which is the subject of chapter 6.

6

Looking for Strength:
The Search for Exceptions

When it gets dark enough, you can see the stars.

Charles Beard

When it is darkest, I find stars in unexpected places.

Problems of any kind vary in their severity, and the extent of any individual problem ebbs and flows. Each has the capacity to overwhelm at times. As problems vary in strength and intensity, the paths to solve them may emerge. Here, the therapist is charged with the responsibility of leading a search for these exceptions—for times when the problem was somehow different. From the search for exceptions comes the last component in the formula for intervention, the homework task.

The *American Heritage Dictionary* defines an exception as "a case that does not conform to the normal rule." In problem situations, an exception is just that: an event that does not conform to the way the problem normally occurs. An exceptional event breaks a rule; somehow it stands out from the rest of the pattern. Once such an exception is identified, the task of the therapist and client is to examine that event against its background and try to see how it occurred. Did the exception just happen spontaneously? Or did the client do something to make the problem vary? Was there a change in how the client thought about the problem or felt toward it? How was the rest of the problem situation affected by this change? The answer to any of these questions may suggest a path to a solution.

When clients come in for therapy, it is often extremely difficult for them to see any variance in the pattern of the problem. They are simply too close to the events, or so caught up in their situation that they feel engulfed in a fabric that wraps them as tightly as a second skin. If no exception is ever identified or explored, the therapeutic discussion can only center around the nature of the problem and its antecedents and causes. While these issues are interesting and can be helpful, this focus in therapy may not have the transforming power that a search for exceptions could provide.

The therapist's job is to help pull back that second skin—to loosen the fabric of the situation so that the client can step away from it and view it in a new way. In this therapy, "pulling the problem back" is done by asking good exception questions.

Context of the Problem

No matter how complex or amorphous a problem may be, the client view when it is first presented in therapy makes it appear to be a solid, indivisible thing. This view can be represented by the smooth, unmarked surface of a hard wooden ball or sphere (figure 6.1).

Fig. 6.1. The client view before exception questions

Asking exception questions about times when the problem was different or a little bit better can markedly change the client's view of the problem. The problem that seemed so solid, so impermeable, now appears to have gaps or openings in it, or areas where the connection between components of the situation are less tightly connected than they first appeared to be. The sphere has holes in it, and parts of it have been broken off or are missing from its surface (figure 6.2).

In each case, the problem lives in a context or a matrix of feelings, thought processes, and behaviors. All of these support the existence of the problem as the client knows it. In the second drawing, the therapist has asked for specific times when

Fig. 6.2. The client view after exception questions

the problem was different, and the client has been able to identify nine times when it was. Each chip in the sphere or hole drilled through it marks the existence of a time when the problem was somehow different.

When exception questions are asked and the client considers them thoughtfully, the usual outcome is as the second drawing shows: holes in the client view of the problem. Note that since the client view of the problem is accepted by the therapist, the exceptions that are found must change how the client views the problem (at least slightly). And even a slight difference in how the client sees the problem offers hope, creates expectation for change, and makes room for a solution.

In Solution-Focused Therapy, exception questions are viewed as *interventions,* whether the client is able to answer them or not. As interventions, these questions have a perturbing and long-lasting provocative power.

Case Note

"I don't know." A woman brought her daughter and her husband, the child's stepfather, for therapy. The presenting problem was that the daughter had accused her stepfather of fondling her. The mother appeared stunned throughout the interview. She either answered all exception questions with "I don't know" or refused to answer them at all. In watching this, my sense was that this was the best she could do at the time. The questions were put out for her consideration and there was no pressure for her to answer or tell her story in a different way.

This same woman returned the following week for a second session. Before the therapist could speak, she stated: "Last week I was stunned by what was going on in my family. I thought about those questions you asked and I have the answers now."

Other clients who were not able to answer questions in the course of telling their stories did not forget them either. In the week that followed their first sessions, they remembered the questions and were ready to offer the answers to them when asked in the next session. Exception questions have much staying power after a session has ended.

Finally, it can be said that the matrix of feelings, thoughts, behaviors, and relationships that support the existence of the problem will not support its opposite, the *solution* to the problem. A change in any of these four areas will set up the potential for change in the other areas and therefore a variance in the problem. When thoroughly explored in therapy, such a variation is often enough to solve the problem.

In the arena of real human problems, it is difficult to predict which change will occur first—a change in either behavior, feelings, thoughts, or relationships. This choice is in the client's hands. The therapist can only wait and watch for the choice that each client makes.

Exploring for Exceptions

Exceptions may appear naturally in the course of a session, or the therapist may need to request examples of these in relation to the problem. In conversation, clients use a number of words and phrases to indicate that a condition varies. Such "clue" words include the following:

every now and then	once in a while
gradually	many times
most of the time	periodically

rarely	frequently
likely	usually
sometimes	occasionally
often	almost never or almost always
seldom	hardly
infrequently	probably

All of these words indicate that the condition or situation or problem being discussed has a tendency to vary in some way. Along with the numerous other words in the English language that indicate a change or fluctuation, these words are actually gifts to the therapist who looks for times when the problem is different.

Case Note

What was different? *A couple came in for therapy at the Brief Family Therapy Center. With Insoo Berg as the supervisor behind a one-way mirror, the couple and I were entering the therapy room when the wife screamed at her husband:*

> *Wife:* If only you were like you were before we got married, we wouldn't have the problems we have now! *(Pointing to him in a menacing way)*

> *Therapist (sitting down):* What would you like to be different as a result of coming to therapy?

> *The supervisor immediately interrupted the session by buzzing for a conference.*

> *Supervisor:* Ask them what *was* different about him before they were married.

An exception had already been introduced at the very beginning of the session. I have learned since then to avoid having expectations of how material containing exceptions will be introduced by a client. I listen for clue words and ask questions about exceptions related to the therapy goal at any time during a session when there is an opportunity or a need to do so.

The purpose of exploring for exceptions is to look for times when the problem had less of an impact or has changed in some way. It does not matter whether the change occurs because the client has made a difference in the problem through some effort of his or her own or the client is unsure how the change happened to occur. In any case, clients need to be questioned in order to explore these differences; otherwise, as a general rule they will not think to delve deeper into the nature of the exception and its implications for their problem. Without a focus on exceptions, the therapist and client are likely to concentrate on discussing the problem, its exact nature and probable causes, and so on; this is especially true if either one or both of them is at all fascinated with the type of problem that is theirs to solve.

According to the work of deShazer and Berg (1991), there are two types of exceptions: deliberate exceptions and spontaneous ones. Both types have a role to play in Solution-Focused Therapy.

Deliberate Exceptions

A deliberate exception is a change in the problem that the client somehow introduces, often after much frustration with trial and error. The key point is that the client wills this change—he or she thinks or feels or does something that can be repeated, counted, measured, or observed. At some level of consciousness, the client has considered making this change and then tried it (and clients usually do feel as if a deliberate exception is at least partially under their control). The change may not necessarily feel like an answer to the problem; in fact, even though a deliberate strategy may have met with some success in the past, clients often overlook its importance and may have tried it only one or two times. Because the change is an intentional one, it is something that the client *can* repeat and see if it continues to help.

Often, where there is one deliberate exception, there are others. It is the therapist's task to begin and continue the search for deliberate exceptions. If there are many deliberate exceptions, the problem may move quickly toward solution. (Some clients are aware that they are close to solving a problem; others are not.) Even if a problem seems close to being solved, this prospect usually dawns on clients slowly in a way and at a pace that is uniquely their own.

Deliberate exceptions may involve feelings, thoughts, or behavior. All three elements share the common characteristics of being measurable and repeatable.

Case Note

Dora. *The stated goal of Dora, the client who had been diagnosed as being both addicted to medication and suffering from clinical depression, was to "be happier." When asked what she would be doing differently at the time in the future when she was less depressed, she listed these activities:*

1. Visiting shut-ins

2. Singing in her church choir

3. Walking daily

4. Telling herself to feel differently

5. Spending time with her husband

6. Doing volunteer work at a local hospital

7. Watching favorite TV shows

8. Reading a new book

When asked about the times when her depression was not as bad, she volunteered that she was already doing a number of the activities on her list. Since she clearly did not view these exceptions as an indication that her depression was close to being solved, I continued to accept her view of the problem and how she saw herself handling it. Together we continued to explore the various ways that she was able to make a difference in the problem she faced.

Therapist: When is your depression not so bad?

Dora: It is *so* bad. Always here. Been here for twenty years. *(Whispering)*

Therapist: So there are no times when it is a little bit better?

Dora: Well, it is not so bad when I visit other people. I just forget about it for a while. The shut-ins need so many things, you know.

Therapist: Yes, that's true. How does a visit to shut-ins help you?

Dora: When I get out, I don't think about it as much. I am okay when I am in the choir on Sundays, I guess.

Therapist: How does that help?

Dora: Well, I am thinking of someone else—not me.

Therapist: What else helps—even a little bit?

Dora: When I sing I forget how sad I am. How long it's been since I really felt good.

Therapist: Really? How does this help?

This interview continued in a similar way until eight deliberate exceptions were named. (In reviewing the list, the reader will see that all eight activities are measurable and repeatable.) Note that exploring these exceptions with her is very different from trying to persuade her that her problem was nearly solved. She simply did not see it that way, and such an approach on the therapist's part would have insulted her knowledge and generated significant resistance from her. Most likely, it would take several more sessions before she was ready to acknowledge that her depression had lifted more than "only slightly."

Spontaneous Exceptions

A "spontaneous" exception is a variation in the problem condition that appears to just "pop up" unexpectedly, without any apparently recognizable cause. To the client, such a mystifying change feels like a chance event or an act of God. Most importantly, it does not appear to be connected to his or her effort; since the exception seems to be a fluke that "just happened," it appears useless as a means to solve the problem. The following cases contain examples of the kind of discussion that typically occurs between client and therapist regarding spontaneous exceptions.

Case Notes

Client: "The problem is better when my husband isn't home, and I never know when that will be."

Therapist: When is another time that you noticed that the problem of worry isn't so bad?

Client: When I get some time alone. That isn't very often, you understand.

Therapist: Yes, I do understand. What are you doing when your husband isn't home or when you are alone that helps you?

Client: I try to meditate.

Therapist: How does this help?

Another example:

Client: It is different when all of my relatives come for a visit, but that is only once a year.

Therapist: What was different at that time?

Client: Things were just better between my daughter and me. I don't know.

Therapist: When was the last time things were just a little bit better between Carla and you?

Client: We got along for about two hours last Saturday. That isn't much. We can usually get along for a few minutes—sometimes.

Therapist: How were you able to do that last Saturday for as long as two hours?

Client: I counted to ten before I said anything to her.

Therapist: How does this help?

Another example:

Client: I notice he is much better when the weather changes.

Therapist: Really? What is happening then?

Client: When it is cooler, he gets along much better.

Therapist: What is he doing then that helps him?

Client: Well I know that he walks some and the air is easier for him to breathe.

Therapist: Really? How does this help?

Another example:

Client: I am better when I can walk around, but I can never tell when I will feel like doing that.

Therapist: What is better for you when you are walking around?

Client: I feel more alive, like I have hope or something. I like to try to wash dishes or clothes if I can muster the energy.

Therapist: What helps you to get the energy to do that?

Client: I have to tell myself that it is disgusting to stay in bed all day long. I have to get sick of what I am doing.

Therapist: What does it take for you to get sick of what you are doing?

Client: I have to see how much time has passed.

Therapist: How does this help?

In each example, the therapist's questions help to transform a spontaneous exception into a deliberate one or to uncover an aspect of the experience that is within the client's control. Since clients rarely make this transition on their own, it is the therapist's job to ask questions designed to bring out anything that clients think, feel, or do that contributes to the difference that they have observed.

Often clients cannot identify anything that they have done, and their attitude toward the exception seems somewhat hopeless. It is important for the therapist to stay with the attitude of the client and not take the lead at this point. Selling hope to a client who is not sure that change is really possible may be construed as an insult; such a conflict will not arise if the therapist stays with and respects the client's mood and language. Whatever the client's view of self and the problem is, stay with that view.

What the therapist can do is to help the client pinpoint how a difference in the problem condition occurred. It is in this difference that a repeatable solution may be found.

Questions to Find Exceptions

There is a pattern to follow when asking good exception questions. The more closely this pattern is followed, the more likely it is that a deliberate exception will be found and that additional exceptions will be brought to light once an area of client strength is uncovered. This pattern of questioning digs out client strength from wherever it was hidden. Such an exploration can be a pleasant surprise to the client.

The pattern contains three simple questions:

1. When was the problem a little better?

2. What did you do (or think or feel) that helped at that time?

3. How did this help?

This trio needs to be asked each time the client volunteers an exception related to the therapy goal or is asked to identify one by the therapist. Since a word-for-word repetition of these questions sounds mechanical, I use clients' words and bits of their sentences and weave the three questions in with their way of discussing the problem.

Here is a partial list of the kinds of questions that I use to begin a search for exceptions to the problem condition.

- Are there times when the problem is a bit different?

- When was the last time you noticed a difference in the problem?

- Are there times when the problem feels a little bit better?

- Are there times when you think (*or feel or act*) differently about this problem?

- The last time the problem was better, what were you doing (*or thinking or feeling*) differently?

Different clients may be helped by examining the problem situation from either a cognitive orientation or from the perspective of feelings or in terms of changes in behavior. Regardless of the perspective, each of these opening questions is followed by the second and third questions in the pattern. Some variations of follow-up questions include:

- What were you doing (*or feeling or thinking*) differently at that time?

- How did you come up with that idea?

Another version of this same question is:

- How did you allow yourself that feeling?

The third question asks: "How did this help you?" Taken together, these questions appear as follows:

The last time you noticed a difference in the problem, what were you
doing (*or feeling or thinking*) differently? What was better at that time?
How did this help you?

It is helpful to use these questions in the sequence presented, and it is particularly important to weave them into the client's conversation. Although the questions serve as guidelines for moving the therapy along, a rigid application of them is not recommended—in part, because such an approach can sound forced, and, more importantly, because hearing the client's story is still the therapist's primary objective here. The therapist should also make sure that the exception questions focus on areas related to the stated goal of the therapy.

By inserting exception questions wherever possible as clients tell their stories, the therapist helps to assure that clients are given credit for any progress toward the resolution of the therapy goal, no matter how small that progress might be. In session, the questions help both therapist and client become more attentive as soon as a bit of progress appears; they achieve the objective of highlighting each positive change as it occurs, until all the progress can be recounted at the end of the session.

Case Note

Dora. *Dora had the view that she was basically ineffective in working on her depression and that few things had helped. The therapist accepted her view of herself and the little bit of progress she felt she had made and persisted in looking for exceptions. The questions asked focused on her continued depression, the deliberate exceptions she came up with in relation to her goal, and her view of herself as she worked on her goal. This excerpt from the interview reveals the therapist's strategy in all three areas.*

> *Dora:* I tried all the things you said to do. (*Giving credit to the therapist for her work*)
>
> *Therapist:* Well, how did all that stuff work for you?
>
> *Dora:* I am still so depressed.
>
> *Therapist:* I see. Since you are still so depressed *(accepting client's view as valid for her)*, which of the things that you tried helped you the most, do you think?
>
> *Dora:* I guess getting out of the house. I'm just not strong enough to do a lot of that, you know.
>
> *Therapist:* When did you get yourself out of the house?
>
> *Dora:* Three times. To go to church on Sunday, to choir practice, and out to dinner with my husband. It only helped a little bit. I still feel so blue.
>
> *Therapist:* What does feeling "so blue" mean to you?
>
> *Dora:* I have to do something with this depression. I can't just let it go.
>
> *Therapist:* Of course. What else helped you even a little bit this week?
>
> *Dora:* I went out to my garden to pick some flowers for dinner.

One curious aspect of this case was that Dora kept this view of herself and her progress right up until the last session, when she declared that her depression had improved. These were her views and they were crucial to her. The therapist's job was to stay with these views and move in synch with her pace.

Exception Questions for Problem Relationships

Solution-Focused Therapy views problems as existing in relationships, and most clients either report that relationships affect the problems in their lives or view their relationships as the cause of the problems they experience. Either way, when clients present their problems as being attached to or caused by another person, I use questions that are relationship oriented and aimed at finding client strength in individuals and within their relationships.

The first assumption I make about any couple is that they are coming to therapy to keep the relationship. If I see any reason to question this premise, I ask each their goal for coming to therapy. I may separate them for this purpose, if I think that either one might be intimidated by the other's presence. At times, clients do come to therapy to end relationships, and that is a reasonable goal to have, since therapy can help a couple separate in practical and predictable ways.

The questions used with partners differ only slightly from those used with individuals. Since one partner's behavior affects the other, the questions can either be aimed at the individual's own response or the individual's response in relation to the partner. In either case, these questions address the system that is their relationship. Here are some examples.

To wife:

- The last time your husband drank less, what was he doing differently? *(Relationship question)*

- What were you doing differently? *(Individual question)*

- How did this help? *(Individual question)*

- What would he say you were doing differently that helped him? *(Relationship question)*

To husband:

- The last time you were drinking less, what were you doing differently? *(Individual question)*

- What was your wife doing differently? *(Relationship question)*

- What would your wife say you were doing differently? *(Relationship question)*

- How did your actions help her to change? *(Relationship question)*

There are many variations of these questions; the content of each comes from each unique client and the situation that she or he is facing. Each type of question either focuses on the relationship itself or on the individuals who have created and continue to define the relationship. It is important to include both types of question, because the answers give the therapist a clear picture of what is happening that needs to change. The problem, whatever it is, lies in the relationship between the partners. It is their relationship and their view of what it looks like to them that is the unit for treatment.

Moreover, the therapist must enter their world as carefully as he or she enters the world of an individual client. The therapist must identify each client's individual views, strengths to compliment, and homework tasks to perform. Each of these items will differ from person to person.

Beginning therapists sometimes feel that the therapy work will be easier to do if the partners see things the same way and have agreed on their goals for therapy. My experience tells me that a marked agreement on the goal and in how each partner views the problem is often a signal that one partner (or both) may feel forced or obligated into agreeing with the other.

I approach each partner in the same way: by honoring the words that they say. Doing so leads to client cooperation; as in individual therapy, this is the path of least resistance for the therapist. And relationships have surprising healing qualities. The same aspects of themselves that brought the partners together in the first place surface again and again to help them heal themselves and their patterns of relating.

Unclaimed resources in relationships. Whether the clients are partners or parents and children, even the most troubled relationships have numerous untapped resources to draw on. The therapist need only be willing to leave room for some flexibility in her or his own ideas about what is helpful to see these unused strengths. Once again, it may help to see things "upside down" and find a use for behavior that is typically regarded as "bad" or inappropriate.

A good example of an opportunity for finding an unexpected resource in an intimate relationship occurs each of those many times when partners who have come in for therapy start to blame each other for their problems. Rather than view blaming as a trap, I look at it as a manifestation of each partner's focused effort to keep track of what's going on between them. Similarly, the anger that usually accompanies a round of charges and countercharges can be viewed as a measurement of the concern that the partners have: the more heated the partners seem to be about an issue, the more invested they are in that issue. When blaming and anger are redefined as "keeping track of what's going on" and "a heavy investment in an issue," clients tend to feel that the therapist has understood their points of view.

In heated blaming situations, each partner tends to be exclusively focused on the problematic aspects of the relationship; even so, this negative focus can be viewed as a potential resource. By introducing the same kinds of exception questions, the attention and energy that the partners devote to blaming each other can be redirected to the task of using their tracking skills to find anything that is helping either of them in their relationship. Note that the effort is to have them change only the behaviors that they track, and not the tracking itself. Essentially, tracking is just a skill that each partner has; as such, it is a necessary component of the way they relate to each other, with each of them keeping track of numerous details in their lives. Seen this way, a frustrating symptom can be used to support the growth of anything that is working well in the relationship.

Ultimately, whatever happens in the therapy room is a resource—a clue that gives meaning to the client's world and suggests the next steps to take. Yet many therapists find it a struggle to see such things as crying, worry, and self-sacrifice as resources. I remind myself that the only barrier is my own thinking; all that is required is to relax my definition of the word "resource." When I think I'm seeing trouble, I've trained myself to turn my thoughts upside down, and, more often than not, the resource I'm looking for appears.

It's a relatively straightforward switch for most of us to see crying as "a normal, expected response to hurt." Other troubling behaviors, thoughts, and feelings may need a greater effort. Here is a partial list of questions you can try asking yourself when you're tempted to label client responses in a negative way:

Is *heated debate* a sign of *intense concern*?

Does a client's *refusal to move* reflect *a necessary caution*?

Does *a lack of trust* in a relationship indicate *a need to rebuild and start over*?

Is the client's *shock* actually *an understandable response to trauma*?

Are *feelings of numbness* actually *an expected response to shock*?

Do the client's *thoughts of self-harm* signal *a need for immediate protection*?

Case Note

Husband (yelling and pointing to his wife): She nags the hell out of me. I am not that bad a guy or husband. I do my best. She just can't see it.

Wife (retorting in an equally loud voice with pointing gestures): Oh, right—like you remember your part in any agreement we make. *(Pleading)* You can't even hear what is so important to me. I feel so frustrated.

Therapist: What is it that has to be different for you? *(Goal question to husband)*

Husband: She has to stop nagging—I just can't stand it anymore. She never used to be this way.

Therapist: When she was different, what was she doing instead? *(Making use of exception introduced by husband)*

Husband: She asked me to do things instead of insisting and screaming.

Therapist: How do you think she was able to do that?

Husband: She took her time and listened to me.

Therapist: And how did that help?

Husband: When she listened to me, I started to listen to her too.

Therapist (to husband): What do you think she would say you were doing differently that helped her to listen instead of nagging? *(Relationship exception question)*

Husband (puzzled): I guess she would say I did more to help her.

Therapist (to wife): Is he right?

Wife: Maybe, I don't know. He wasn't always this bad.

Therapist: Oh? When was he not so bad? *(Using client words and exception introduced by wife)*

Wife: When he did not work so much. I know he's tired, but I've got the kids, and I'm tired too.

Therapist: Yes, you are, aren't you? *(Accepting client view)* In your situation, what has to change for you? *(Goal question)*

Wife: He has to help more, or by God I'll throw him out on the street.

Therapist: When was the last time you caught him helping out a little more?

Wife (stunned): Well . . . maybe last Wednesday night. He looked over Tom's homework.

Therapist: Really? Did he do this on his own, or did you do something that helped him to do this?

Wife: Just asked him, that's all.

Therapist: That's all it took?

Wife: Yes.

Husband: No. It was the way you asked me. And you listened to me talk, too.

Therapist (to husband): What was different about the way she asked that time?

Husband: She listened to me, then she asked me calmly.

Therapist (to wife): Is he right?

Wife: I think so.

Therapist: How did this help?

The therapist's focus in this session was to get the partners to use their "blaming" skills to focus on times that may have escaped their notice when things were a little better. The therapist follows the partners' lead, using their words and accepting their views and using individual questions and relationship questions to ask for reports on when things were different. These reports come from both angles on the relationship, from wife and husband, as both are individually asked to comment on themselves and on how each relates to the other.

In this case, the partner's goals are different and yet connected. Since they are so watchful of each other's behavior, if either one of them changes, the other will immediately feel the impact of the change. This is the usual case in partner relationships: goals differ, and the partners are mutually affected by each other's behavior.

When partners have different goals. Individuals in relationships rarely see the problems they are having in the same way. It is expected that intimate partners or spouses and parents and their children will each enter therapy with differing agendas. These different agendas in turn will suggest different goals for each individual. *This is a given.*

From my perspective, it is not necessary for each partner to be working on the same goal. If the partners do have the same goal, it does feel easier to reach consensus and to move onto another goal when success has been realized with the first goal.

When persons in relationships have different goals, I remind myself that each partner has a valid world view; the partners are simply looking at their problem from different stances as they respond to the same situation. Each individual goal reflects the reality which that partner is currently experiencing. The work we do together follows from the assumption that working on these individual goals will have the needed effect on the relationship. This is so even if only one person is working on the problem, since experience has shown that a change in any one aspect of a relationship has the potential to make a difference in the relationship system. It sets up a change in the needed direction in the responses of each of the others who surround the person making the change. The change is felt by all, since clients are just as adept at tracking what each of them does well as they are at keeping track of their mistakes. Clients often experience such a change as a natural step in self-correction, something they were moving toward anyway.

The outcome of such an effort can be amazing. If we keep in mind the importance of our valuing their views, finding compliments that fit their self-images well enough, and then asking questions that explore exceptions from a relationship perspective for each of them, the therapy will move forward considerably.

Case Note

*"**Exactly.**" A husband blamed his wife for "nagging" him; she in turn blamed him for "not helping out" enough. While they were able to establish goals for changing these behaviors, each partner stated that the other had to change first—an impasse that felt frustrating to both of them.*

In preparing a written intervention for the couple, the therapist came to the conclusion that this mutual reluctance to "go first" was best viewed "upside down" as "necessary caution," a stance that both partners agreed was their reason for being slow to change. When they heard the term "necessary caution" in the written intervention, both nodded. The wife said, "Exactly."

Getting a list of exceptions from partners. When used with an individual or within a relationship, exception questions yield a number of deliberate or spontaneous exceptions. In order to be most effective, the search for exceptions needs to yield a *list* of exceptions, not just one or two. At first, this task may feel laborious to the therapist, but with practice exception questions can be woven into the conversation with ease.

When working with partners, it is important to get both partners to tell what each was doing (or thinking or feeling) at the time when the problem was a bit better. They know—or at least they think that they know. Certainly they can readily report on themselves and on each other. Note that the partners do not have to agree what either of them did to "make it better." They do not even have to know what either of them is doing when the problem is better. Even when the partners disagree or do not have definite answers, asking exception questions still helps them to focus on when "it" was better.

In fact, with practice and over time, the questions can be posed as sentences that feel more conversational and less interruptive of the natural flow of client conversation. The same questions posed above can be worded in these ways:

For individuals:

- I am wondering about the last time you saw a difference in this problem and how you account for that difference.

- I am curious about was happening the last time you remember the problem being different.

- I am wondering what you did that made it different.

- I would like to know the last time you handled this problem a little bit better. I would like to know what you did (*or thought or felt*) that got it this way.

For persons in relationships:

- I am curious about the last time you remember your husband drinking less. When was that? (*Wait for response.*) I would like to know what he was doing instead. (*Wait for response.*) I would also like to know what he would say you were doing instead. (*Wait for response.*) What do you think he would say you might have done that helped him drink a little less?

- It might be helpful to look at the last times things were just a little bit better for you and what you were doing at that time. (*Wait for response.*) I wonder what your daughter (*or husband or wife or son or lover*) would say you did differently that might have helped the situation to be better at that time.

- The last time things were going just a little bit better—what were you doing differently? (*Wait for response.*) I wonder what you would say your husband was doing differently at that time. (*Wait for response.*) I wonder what your husband would say you were doing differently.

Finding Homework Tasks from Exception Questions

As we have seen, exceptions can be divided into those that are deliberate and those that are spontaneous. Since deliberate exceptions by definition can be repeated by the client at will, it seems reasonable to conclude that the more deliberate exceptions there are in a client's situation, the closer the client is to solving her or his problem. In contrast, when most of the exceptions on a client's list are spontaneous ones that cannot readily be repeated by the client, the further he or she is from solving the problem at hand.

This is a sensible conclusion; when clients can generate repeatable changes that reduce the impact of the problem, then they are liable to solve the problem more readily. Clients, however, do not always have the perception that the problem is close to being solved, even when it appears to be so to the therapist or to others in the client's life. And when a client's perception is that the problem is more out of control than in control, usually the problem is less likely to reach an immediate resolution.

Two factors help clients to realize how close they may be to a solution: (1) well-worded exception questions related to the therapy goal and (2) a recount of progress at the end of each session. A list of exceptions, then, becomes an imperative in this therapy. From this list comes the homework task, which generally reflects the dominant type of exception on the client's list.

Homework tasks for deliberate exceptions. If the client has more deliberate exceptions than spontaneous ones, then the homework task is simply to do more of what is already working (and to take any other positive steps that come to mind). As more deliberate exceptions are added to the original list in later sessions, some older tasks will drop off as the client finds them less effective over time. Other more powerful exceptions usually replace them.

Even though either partners or individuals have many deliberate exceptions, clients may not see how close they are to solving their problem; they may have to live with the changes in their situation for a time before they can recognize improvements and acknowledge how close they are. In any case, clients are always asked to come back and report on progress in the next session as part of the homework task. Adding this task also requires the therapist to check on progress toward the therapy goal in each session.

Here is an example of how a task is worded for a client working on anger control who had many deliberate exceptions.

> What I would like for you to do this week is to do all the things that
> have helped even a little, such as running, walking, breathing deeply,
> counting to ten, and talking about your anger with Jane. Come back
> and tell me which one worked best and if you found any other things
> to do that helped. Does that fit?

Homework tasks for spontaneous exceptions. If there are more spontaneous exceptions than deliberate ones, then the client's task is simply to (1) try to repeat or find a way to increase anything that has worked even a little bit and (2) do anything else that he or she deems reasonable to help the situation. When nothing has worked or there are only a few spontaneous exceptions, clients are asked to return home and study themselves for a week to see how they got through the problem. Either way, clients are sent out to study themselves and figure out what they are actually doing to cope with their current situation.

Here is an example of a task where a number of deliberate exceptions are present.

> I'd like you to try the things that have worked a little bit already and
> pay attention to what else helps you. And I'd like you to come back
> and tell me about it next week. Does that seem reasonable?

Here is a task for a case where only one deliberate exception is present.

I understand that walking may have helped you this week, and I also see that not much else has worked. So, what I would like you to do is to continue walking when you feel like it, and I'd like you to pay attention to the times when the problem of your anger is a little bit better this week and then come back and tell me what made the difference. Does that seem reasonable?

In this case, no deliberate exceptions are present.

I understand that nothing helped this week at all. So, I'd like you to pay very close attention to the times next week when there is any difference in your anger—even if the difference is very small. And I'd like you to come back and tell me what you did that made that difference. Does that work okay for you?

If the number of spontaneous and deliberate exceptions is about the same, both tasks are combined: the client is asked to repeat each of the things that worked and to continue to pay attention to spontaneous changes in the situation. Once again, the therapist also asks the client to be ready to report back which things worked best and to provide more information about anything else that helps.

Here is an example of a task for a client who had three deliberate exceptions and three spontaneous ones.

I'd like for you to try running, walking, and counting to ten to help with the problem of anger, especially since you found that these three things already help some *(deliberate exceptions)*. I would also like you to watch and see if your anger is different when the weather is different, or when you don't know when your husband will come home, or if relatives choose to visit *(spontaneous exceptions)*. I need more information about which of these things worked best for you. Does that feel right to you?

There are two reasons why clients are very willing to try these options. First, their own ideas about what has already worked are being supported. Even if there has been only minimal progress, their efforts and strengths are both being affirmed and put to work for them.

Second, the homework task follows the client view and compliments in the written intervention. This is a time of high levels of concentration and cooperation; the client has felt that the therapist has "heard" him or her, and the therapist offers compliments that the client sees as true. All three components are offered in the client's language and use bits and pieces of what is already working.

This is not a difficult "sell" for the therapist; the wisdom underlying the task has come from within the client, and the experience is an affirming one, from start to finish. Only on rare occasions has this approach not worked well. In retrospect, those occasions seemed to occur because I misunderstood or misinterpreted the client view, which is the main focus of the client's attention. (Usually this happens when my own attention is distracted by secondary issues in the client's talk that engage my personal interest. Chapter 8 will outline some strategies to deal with distracting elements in sessions.)

One last word: I always ask clients if the assignment fits or makes sense to them. If I have successfully read and repeated the client view, picked compliments that the client agrees with, and used appropriate material from their exceptions for the task, I rarely experience a poor "fit." On the rare occasion that I do, I readily accept the corrections that the client offers when the written intervention is offered. On the spot, I renegotiate the homework task, incorporate any elements that the client tells me will fit better, and ask for a report on that the following week.

With the three elements of the intervention in place, then, the next chapter offers a format for writing the intervention and delivering it to the client and some suggestions on how to use the intervention in session.

7

Interventions

Everything in this book could be wrong.

Richard Bach

Or very likely it could all be rearranged and make more sense.

When teaching the Solution-Focused Therapy model, I encourage students and others learning it to begin using it any way they can. For some, this means learning to write compliments first. Others find it easier to start with the client view, and still others begin by listing exceptions. Whether these choices are simply individual preferences or a result of some other factor probably does not matter. So long as the therapist feels comfortable with the components of the model already learned, he or she will be able to move forward in his or her own unique way.

What really does matter is understanding how these three parts work together for the benefit of the client. The therapist needs to see a pattern in the style of interviewing and must be able to use the components of the formula in a repeatable format for every session. The formula and the format for its use will remain much the same from client to client and session to session; only the contents of the written intervention vary according to the client's situation. Both the formula and the format for a written intervention will be presented in this chapter, along with examples of their use. In addition, suggestions for conducting the session and a sample form for making progress notes are offered.

Progress Notes

For review, the components of the formula are as follows:

Intervention = Client view + client compliments + homework task

For every session, with every client, each of these elements is identified. The therapist spends much time asking questions to access this information, and throughout the session the therapist remains curious about the client's view of the situation, the client's coping skills, and what the client believes that she or he does well in relation to the problem at hand. The therapist waits expectantly for information about any of these to emerge in the client's story or to come as a response to questions. As we have seen, the task is to highlight anything that helps the client toward the contracted therapy goal. Once an area of strength is highlighted, the therapist makes sure that there is much discussion about it and how it might be a clue to the solution.

Progress Notes

Client name _____ Date _____ Session _____

Unique phrases and words (client view)

1. _____

2. _____

3. _____

4. _____

Compliments

1. _____

2. _____

3. _____

4. _____

Deliberate exceptions _____

_____

_____

Spontaneous exceptions _____

_____

_____

Number and type of exceptions _____

_____

_____

Intervention(s) (from client view, compliments, and exceptions) _____

_____

_____

_____

_____

_____

_____

_____

_____

_____

To assist in the collection of these bits of information, some kind of a format for making progress notes in session is needed. Therapists and students often change the basic format presented here to fit their own individual styles and needs, but most find that a form containing all of these elements helps train them to collect the needed information.

Notetaking is a basic therapy skill that will become a habit with time and practice. This form serves as a reminder for how the therapist is to listen and take notes. Remember that it is important to use the client's own words when recording notes on this form. Record unique, emotionally charged phrases, compliments that the client believes to be true, and any exceptions that are helping in any way to meet the therapy goal.

Writing an Intervention

The format for organizing the information collected as progress notes into a written intervention has minor variations, but essentially remains the same regardless of the client's problem or presentation of it. Of course, the contents of each intervention will vary from client to client—and from session to session, due to changes in the client view and as progress is made toward the therapy goal. The format serves as a prototype for writing any intervention in this style of therapy.

The key feature overall is that all three elements of the formula—the client view, compliments, and homework task—must each make sense to the client and match the client's own sense of her or his situation.

In paragraph form, the format for a written intervention is as follows:

Because you think *(insert the client view—four phrases that the client used to describe the problem)*

1. _____

2. _____

3. _____

4. _____

I am impressed with *(insert three to four compliments)*

1. _____

2. _____

3. _____

4. _____

What I'd like for you to do is *(insert task for either deliberate exceptions, spontaneous exceptions, or a combination of the two)*

_____

_____

_____

and come back and tell me how it went.

I always follow my reading of the intervention with the question, "How does this fit for you?" and wait for the client to tell me how it fits.

Other beginning phrases include "Since it seems to you ..." or "Because it is clear to you that. ..." When a client or clients are experiencing an internal conflict or facing two choices or considering several alternatives, it is important to start the intervention with a phrase that matches that conflict. A workable phrase for this kind of intervention is "Part of me thinks along with the part of you that thinks ... while the other part of me thinks like the other part of you that thinks. ..." The key again is to match the material that the client has presented.

Other beginning phrases for the compliment part of the intervention include "I am really struck by ..." "I can really appreciate ..." "I am amazed that ..." and "I respect ...."

I generally use the opening phrase "What I'd like for you to do is ..." for the task section. The tasks are always unique for each client—even for clients who have the same problems—and different from week to week as progress is made.

Using this format may seen a bit awkward at first, but with time and practice the pattern reflected in these words and phrases becomes a way of thinking and doing. Note that keeping to the format is especially important with multiple clients in the same session, since the therapist must repeat the same steps for every client present. My experience has been that I can repeat the format for five people as easily as I can for one. I collect the same information for each client and my notes are correspondingly longer, but clients like hearing about themselves and so tend to be patient with the repetition involved. Each waits with anticipation ("She said something good about him, so I wonder what she'll say about me") while the others have their turn.

Case Notes

A couple with different goals. A husband blamed his wife for "nagging" him, while she in turn blamed him for "not helping out" enough; each partner noted only a couple of times when their problem was better and seemed reluctant to try anything new. Here are their written interventions.

Therapist (to husband): Since you know you are not a bad guy or a bad husband, and you also know that your wife just can't see you do your best, I am amazed that you went with along with the idea of coming here with her for therapy and also that you remember when she was not this way. I am also impressed that you look for reasons why she is the way she is now. I think your caution about wanting her to go first in changing might just be a good idea. So what I want you to do is pay attention to the times when you are feeling more willing to help out. I need to know what she is doing at the time that makes you want to help her. Also watch for times when she is not nagging, and see what she is doing instead and what you are doing too.

Husband: I can do that.

Therapist (to wife): And for you, since you are tired and have the kids and all, and since he can't even hear what is important to you, I am amazed that you can remember when he was different or that you got his help by just asking him. I am impressed that you are so willing to work on this frustrating problem, given that there are times when you want to throw him out on the street. It is a good thing for you to be cautious in changing. I think you have some power in the way you ask things. So, this week, I would like for you to take note of all the times he goes along with your requests and all the times he doesn't and see if you can tell what helps to go along with some and not with others.

Wife: Yes, okay, I will watch him.

Therapist: Good, that's what we need. *(To both)* How does this fit for you?

Husband: It's okay with me. Do we come in at the same time next week?

Wife: Yes, that's a good time.

The intervention for each partner reflects that client's view (compare with the dialogue given in the Case Note for this couple in chapter 6), and the compliments given fit their views. Finally, the tasks assigned make use of the blaming that these partners do with each other. They are already keeping count of each other's wrong-doing; they may as well put that skill to good use. Here, that good use is tracking any moments when they are doing better. The couple agreed to do the work assigned and readily set up another appointment.

An individual client with many deliberate exceptions. *Carla appeared for therapy with a problem of anger. She stated that this had been a problem for many years and was linked to her memory that her father had sexually abused her and her two sisters. Her goal for therapy was to learn to control her anger, state what she wanted, and not be diverted from her needs.*

Carla: I am just as likely to give in to someone else's needs as I am to take care of my own. I have only grown a little in this area.

Therapist: Really? How were you able to do that?

Carla: I'm not sure.

Therapist: When was the last time that you were faced with this kind of decision—I mean, to take care of your own needs or someone else's?

Carla: Uh, last Sunday night all my friends wanted to go out to a late movie, and I really was too tired, but I went anyway. The next day at work I was really tired. I suffer a lot when I do not have enough sleep.

Therapist: So that's an example of a time when you gave in. When was a time when you took care of yourself and that felt right to you?

Carla: It's not like I never do it. Your question sounds like I never do it.

Therapist: Okay, when was a time that you took care of yourself in a way that pleased you?

Carla: One night last week I was tired and I made myself go to bed early.

Therapist: How were you able to do that?

Carla: I think I was just so tired. . . . No, I talked to my closest friend and told her that I could not stay up any longer. I said to her, "I need my rest."

Therapist: So, realizing it and then telling your closest friend helped. How did that help?

Carla: I don't think I got so angry—not like I did when I didn't get enough rest.

Therapist: When was another time?

Carla: I do it . . . I think everytime I shop for groceries and buy the food specified by my diet. I think also when I exercise and do my meditation, and that is four times a week.

Therapist: How were you able to do those things?

Carla: I just think about what is good for me before I do them. Sometimes I have to make myself do it—like exercise.

Therapist: How does this help you?

Carla: I can see a difference in how mad I am when I try to take care of myself. I'm doing something that no one ever did for me.

Therapist: Right. What else helped?

Carla: Well, exercise. . . .

Therapist: How do you make yourself exercise?

Carla: I look at the picture of the way I want to look. It is on the refrigerator, and when I see it, it helps me to get moving.

Therapist: Are you more or less angry when you do these things?

Carla: For sure, less angry. When I take care of what I need, I am not mad at everyone who did not take care of me. But it seems slower than I want.

Therapist: I am sure that is true.

Carla has listed several deliberate exceptions—things she has noticed herself doing that have helped her take care of herself. (These are some of the core issues of recovery from sexual abuse.) Here is the intervention written for her in this session:

Therapist: Since it seems you are just as likely to take care of yourself as you are to take care of someone else, and because you have grown a little in this area, I am impressed at the ways you've come up with to help you decide which one to do—ways like taking time to talk to a friend or thinking about what you need and how much a lack of sleep will cause you to suffer. It seems that you are growing in this area. So, I think I need some more information about how you are growing. What I'd like for you to do is try all the things you have just told me that helped: thinking about what you need, talking to a friend, eating right, going to sleep when you realize you are too tired, exercising, and looking at that picture of yourself. Come back and tell me which worked best for you in controlling your anger and taking care of yourself. How does that fit for you?

This client responded by immediately agreeing with the task and promising a report the following week. She returned with three more deliberate exceptions and an increased sense that she was working very hard on control of anger.

In Carla's case, she expressed her agreement with the intervention by nodding her head vigorously and stating, "Okay, I can do that." It is not unusual for client responses to include laughter or tears or phrases like "Yes, you got it, you know what I've been dealing with." Often the compliments in the intervention will prompt children and teenagers to interrupt with the words "Do you want me to tell you what else I do well?"

It is important to remember that the intervention is an affirming moment (for both client and therapist). Throughout the session, it is our job as therapists to work very hard to honor whatever the client brings into the therapy room and to honor each client right where we find them. The attention and respect that we offer may be the first and only instance of this kind of affirmation that an individual has experienced for some time. Such an affirmation is a reminder of the potentially healthy connections that human beings can make and of the collective wisdom that comes from our interaction.

Using the Intervention in Session

The intervention in a solution-focused approach is written, and I usually take a break to write it. (It is not necessary to break to do this, once one has gained experience in taking notes in session and in delivering the intervention.) The break comes at forty-five minutes after the hour and lasts from five to ten minutes. Before leaving the room, the therapist asks, "Is there anything else I need to know before we finish today?" (Or, if a team has been observing the session, the therapist can ask, "Is there anything else that you think I need to know today before I talk to the team?") Once the client has responded, the therapist stands to leave. The client may also take a break or remain in the therapy room.

If a team has been observing the session, the team will have taken notes similar to those of the therapist's. In comparing notes, the therapist and members of the observing team review the client view, compliments, and types of exceptions, discuss the client's path to date, and work on an intervention that fits. When the team discussion is over, the therapist and the client return and seat themselves in the therapy room.

There is an air of expectation in the room just before the intervention is shared with the client. This moment of hearing client strengths is a stirring one; it captivates all who are present. Although practiced therapists can deliver an intervention without reading it, the fact that the intervention is read to the client adds to the impact it has and makes it sound like an important message. More often than not, clients leave with the feeling that they have experienced something unique. I believe that the overall sense they have is "You have been with me in such a way that I leave feeling better than when I came in. For some reason, you seem to believe in me."

What clients say in response to the intervention is often touching; over the last six years, I have found their responses to being heard the most telling part of this work. It seems that people in general just do not care to listen to the heart of another's message. The honor that is paid to clients' views and the use of their own language leaves them feeling that the therapist has stepped inside their private world and said: "Well, of course this makes sense. What other conclusion could you reach?"

Some of the responses I have heard include the following:

"I didn't think anyone would ever listen to me."

"Thank you for your time and for listening to me. This is the first time I can remember anyone ever doing that."

"Can I come and see you again? I really enjoyed having somebody listen to me."

"I feel you understand me."

"You must know what I am going through."

"I know you have been through the same thing. I can tell by the questions you asked."

"You did pretty good today! Thanks!"

After reading the intervention, the therapist stands right away to move to end the session. Standing symbolizes the end of the therapy session for that day; when other issues arise at this particular moment, these are acknowledged and tabled for the next session. The business affairs of the therapy (collecting fees, setting another appointment) are conducted in another room and are settled before the client leaves.

Case Notes

Zona. *The thirteen-year-old whose problem was an obsession with the rock group New Kids on the Block initially told our counselor that there were no times when the problem was better. The problem was always as bad as the moment she came to therapy. Here is the intervention we wrote for her:*

> *Therapist:* Since it seems to you that you are obsessed with New Kids on the
> Block and that nothing has helped, and especially since your teachers
> and even your mom have given up *(client views)*, it seems to me that
> you could be right, and maybe I cannot help you either. Before I give
> up too, I want you to know that I am amazed that you came in for
> counseling; it's really amazing that you have been able to concentrate at
> all on anything and that you remembered your teachers' and your
> mom's reactions *(compliments she could agree with)*. So, what I'd like for
> you to do—for the next week only—is pay attention to the times when
> you know you are obsessing a little bit less than usual about New Kids
> on the Block and come back to tell me how you handled it.

> *Zona (sighing):* Oh, okay. I gotta help you!

> *Therapist:* Right!

I knew from the nod of her head, her attentiveness to the message, and her agreement to do the task, that the intervention fit well enough. As a team, we had managed to enter her world, see her world her way, and find something useful in it, while not arguing with her view of it. We also chose to have her study herself because there were few deliberate exceptions to begin with; in agreeing with her hopeless attitude, we did so in the hope that she would trade her outlook in for a new one in the near future. I reminded myself and the team that her path was hers and we were following her. We gave up the need to control the outcome and decided only to accompany her as she healed herself.

In her next session, she reported three deliberate exceptions and a slight change in her attitude. She told us that she could change if she "really wanted to." And she did change, in the course of eight sessions, each using the twenty-minute interview. The changes she made were those requested by her mother and teachers and ones that she said she needed to make herself.

Case Note

One day at a time. *A newly sober couple presented for therapy. She had just finished a 28-day stay in an addictions unit in a general hospital, and he had gotten sober in AA. Each had been addicted for about twenty years. Each indicated that remaining sober was their goal for therapy.*

She said that she was really "scared to be with him sober," that she was sure she "didn't know how to do that," and that she "knew what life was like for him" because "I am a drunk myself." She offered other descriptions of her situation, but her body language and tone of voice made it clear that these were the most potent.

For his part, he "was not sure they could remain sober," he knew "he had to go to ninety meetings in ninety days," he "wanted her to want to go to these same meetings," and he was sure he knew "how hard it would be for her in the days ahead." These were his views.

For the therapist, observing the struggle here was very moving. There was an earnest quality in the tone of their voices, and it struck me that they could just as easily be partners in recovery as they had once been enemies in their addictions. The energy they put into harming themselves and their relationship just needed rerouting. I told myself I could not do it for them. They would chart that path themselves if they chose it.

Their overall view was that sobriety was the first order of business for each day, beginning with today. I explored how they had managed to stay sober today with them.

She had read her "Big Book" and her Bible and said the Serenity Prayer many times during that day. She had also called her sponsor. He had done similar things and had separated himself from her when he felt himself getting too angry. They both had attended a meeting for that day.

I went on to explore what they had done to remain sober for the six days prior to the day they came in for therapy. Their exceptions were about the same as the list that each gave before. In addition, each mentioned thinking about the other's struggle and how hard it must be for the other. (I appreciated silently their developing empathy for one another.)

The couple's intervention was a joy to write. The picture of the initial struggles of persons entering recovery after years of addiction was the expected picture. Time after time, this is what we see when addicts get honest and begin their recovery work. It was comforting at the time to remind myself that their focus was today only. It meant that their focus was the manageable one that the Twelve-Step groups encourage: "one day at a time."

Their intervention was as follows:

Therapist (to her): Since you don't know how to be with him sober, and since you see yourself as a drunk who knows what life is like for him *(client view)*, I find it amazing that you are sober right now—and, in fact, that you have been sober for seven days straight and that you are facing the issues that newly recovering persons face head on *(compliments)*. So, what I'd like you to do is to keep doing all the things you have already tried that have helped even a little bit—reading the Bible, reading the Big Book, saying the Serenity Prayer, and calling your sponsor *(deliberate exceptions)*. And I'd like you to pay attention to anything else that helps before our next session and come back and tell me how this worked for you.

Her responses included nodding her head in agreement, saying "Yes, see, that's what I mean," and agreeing to do the task as stated to her.

Therapist (to him): Since you know that you need to remain sober, and that means ninety meetings in ninety days, and also because you know how hard it will be for her in the days ahead *(client view)*, I am very impressed that you let her know your concern about staying sober and that you invited her to go with you to the meetings. It seems to me that you are facing what needs to be faced at this point, by putting staying sober above all else *(compliments)*. And so, what I'd like you to do is to continue all the things you are doing that help you even a little bit—like reading the Big Book and the Bible, saying the Serenity Prayer, calling your sponsor, and especially continuing to separate yourself from her when you are too angry *(deliberate exceptions)*. And I'd like you to pay attention to anything else that helps and come back and tell me how it went.

His nonverbal responses told me I had hit the nail on the head. He teared up when he was praised, nodded his head in agreement with the task, and said, "I think I can do it."

Watching this family beginning to self-correct was quite a moment for me. They did the real work; they faced the tough issues together. It was a blessing just to be there. At the time, I was new to Solution-Focused Therapy, and this couple was a crucial reminder for me of the nature of my role: to follow where I was led, taking note of strength as it appears in any form along the way. The strengths that this couple showed me were just hints of the power they had. They had begun to heal their family and discover the resources of external support and inner wisdom there for them on a path that was clearly their own.

8

Paths to Solution: Structure of Sessions

The journey of a thousand steps begins with the first one.

Lao Tse

The first one is rarely the step we thought it would be.

Once we have let go of the need to know where the client is going with a particular problem, how she or he will solve it, and what steps will be needed to reach that goal, the path to solution is truly in the client's hands. Client and therapist mark this path together as they follow it. To do therapy in this manner, each session must have a similar structure and follow a familiar pattern. Only the content within the structure differs.

In this chapter, the structure of sessions will be outlined, and the pattern for them will be described. Related material covers techniques for dealing with distractions in sessions and identifies a format for presenting cases in staff or professional meetings. Together with thoughts on how a group of therapists can work as a team, useful ways to interact with colleagues who practice different models of therapy will be outlined.

Essentially, solution-focused thinking is the topic here, and its application to cases, colleagues, and self. My experience has been that this way of thinking dovetails well with other professional points of view and personal philosophies.

Structure of Sessions

Most of the discussion that follows describes the structure of the long-interview format of fifty minutes; although the overall structure for a shorter, twenty-minute format is identical, the specific questions developed for that format are described in detail in chapter 12.

In either case, whether I work with a team or alone, I follow the same format in a session, gather the same kinds of information, and organize it in the same way each time. Only the content varies from client to client.

The fifty-minute format. In this format, the interview process that follows the therapist's greeting and the normal social exchanges takes about 45 minutes; the therapist then takes a break from the session to spend time alone considering the case or to work with the team observing the session. Alone or in conference with the team, the therapist considers the client view, compliments, and types of exceptions, and from these three derives a written intervention.

A goal for the whole course of therapy is determined early in the first session, and all sessions focus on this goal until it is solved. Conversation throughout the session is interlaced with exception questions related to the therapy goal.

Working with an observing team. The observing team behind a one-way mirror essentially has the task of collecting the same information that the therapist collects. When the therapist joins the team, the therapist and the team members are each ready to discuss the intervention and to write it together.

The therapist leads the discussion with the team, beginning with this question: What are the client's views? The team then lists these and decides together which views are most critical to use to let the client know that he or she has been understood. If the team cannot agree, then the therapist will make the decision on how to rank the client views.

The therapist writes down the four views selected, organizes them into the paragraph format of the written intervention, and then asks the question: What's going well with the client that the client would agree with and we need to point out? Suggested compliments are read aloud by team members, each making sure the others are using the client's own language.

From three to four compliments are added to the views, and the therapist goes on to ask for exceptions by type and number. As a list of exceptions is drawn up, the team determines how many are deliberate and how many are spontaneous. The list is organized into the last part of the paragraph that makes up the intervention.

The team listens as the therapist reads the intervention for comment; at this point, there may be a minor change or two. This whole process takes less than ten minutes, although a degree of excitement and anticipation that the team usually feels as it works together can sometimes make it difficult to stay on track. When this happens, one of the team members is designated to "tend" the path and keep the discussion focused.

At times, clients have asked to meet the observation team—perhaps sensing something of the growing sense of excitement and hopefulness about change that the team feels as it works. I have always been happy to trust the wisdom of this request and oblige. No matter how bleak a client's situation is, my sense is that meeting a group of professionals who agree that the client is doing a number things well cannot help but be a positive experience.

Case Note

With the team in the room. *In a couple's session, audio equipment failure made it necessary to bring the whole team into the therapy room for the entire session. The team sat on one side of the room, and the therapist and clients sat on the other. There was no break in the session; at 45 minutes after the hour, the team joined the therapist and clients, and the clients observed as we held our usual discussion in front of them. Their responses made it clear that they enjoyed hearing our discussion of their progress and strength.*

In the conference, team members often find it useful to point out to the therapist what is going well in the session and what the therapist is doing to contribute to that progress. This part of the discussion is particularly supportive and nurturing to the therapist; after all, therapists and clients alike are prone to be more attentive when complimented. The team also points out challenges for the therapist, things that the therapist can do more often in the session to heighten client strength. The team may also take a minute during the conference (or later, in a brief post-session discussion) to hear any concerns that the therapist has about his or her own performance.

The team should seek to match the client's mood and presentation of the problem and to support the strengths of both client and therapist. A good match here is crucial to the delivery of the intervention and the client's acceptance of it. Essentially, the team must also trust in client wisdom; the work is simply to weave that wisdom into a useful and fitting intervention.

Working without a team. The therapist working without an observation team still gathers the same information and organizes it in the same way. In my own clinical work, instead of leaving the room, I stop the session at 45 to 50 minutes and take a minute to put the client wisdom back together to formulate the intervention. I signal the client that a message of importance is on the way by asking "Is there anything else I need to know before we finish today?" or "Do I need to know anything else before we close today?" I then change my seating position and tone of voice; from these cues, the client understands that he or she is about to hear the outcome of the session. The intervention follows.

If therapists who work alone can take a break in the session, they will find it helpful to follow the same process used when working with a team. The questions for the therapist to ask himself or herself are:

1. What are the client's views?

2. What things are going well with the client that should be complimented? (Remember that compliments must fit what the client believes to be true.)

3. What kind of exceptions are present and how many of each are there?

4. What is the task?

The therapist then writes the intervention based on the information gathered and returns to offer this to the client.

The teachable moment. With or without the consultation of a team, the therapist will find it helpful to remember that there is no one path that the client must take to solve a problem. Letting go of the outcome of a session may feel intimidating or risky at first, but it is an essential step for the therapist to make. Letting go does make the session an adventure of sorts—an adventure in which the therapist will witness the healing of another person in his or her own unique way.

Throughout the session, the therapist's top priority is to hear the client's story. Good questions will be required, together with acknowledgement of and close attention to any signs that the client says are indications of success.

These elements are all that is necessary to create the "teachable moment" that occurs at the end of every session. In this moment, the clients' wisdom, in whatever amount available, returns to them in their own words, in a form that compliments "a job well done" and encourages more of the fine work they have shown themselves capable of doing.

The twenty-minute format. The twenty-minute format uses a specific set of questions that will be outlined in chapter 12. With or without a team, the process is identical to the fifty-minute session, with the difference that the interview and question period is limted to fifteen minutes, followed by a three-minute break for consultation or deliberation and a two-minute delivery of the intervention.

This format came about when school counselors asked for help in developing a structure for a brief intervention of some kind. Insoo Berg and I examined interview material for the essential questions, and two styles of twenty-minute interview emerged; the style presented in chapter 12 is one that I developed and used with therapy students, who went on to evaluate its use in clinics in Indiana. This format has proved useful in settings where there is limited time, limited staff, transportation problems for clients, or clients frequently arrive late for sessions or present other scheduling problems.

Map of the Session

For both formats, the general map of the session is the same. A specific goal has been set, and the therapist continually asks questions that are in line with the achievement of this goal. These are either exception questions or questions that elicit more information about the client's situation.

Fig. 8.1. How the path alters during the flow of a session

Figure 8.1 provides an image of how the path toward the stated goal alters during the flow of a session. As the client tells his or her story, the exception questions that the therapist weaves in and out of it cannot help but make the situation more hopeful. The more time spent in "exception talk," the more hopeful the situation becomes. This powerful combination of time spent in storytelling and in finding moments when the problem was different seems to solidify change and generate other needed changes. Although the path is "upward," toward the therapy goal, the momentum that this combination generates is like a snowball rolling downhill, gathering strength as it proceeds.

The pattern behind the exception questions that the therapist asks can be seen when they are grouped in this way:

- *When* was it better?

- *What* was better?

- *How* did that improvement happen?

- *What* did you do (*or think or feel*) to make this improvement happen?

- *How* did that help you?

The key to developing a list of exceptions to examine at the session's end is to begin by asking for a number of times *when* the problem was different. For every "when" question, a series of "what" and "how" questions follow. In framing these, it is crucial to stay in the realm that the client presents and to focus on either feeling, thinking, behavior, or relationships.

A major effect of this pattern of questioning is that it leaves the client responsible for change. The role of the therapist is to "hold the light" and point out any signs of progress toward the goal—by probing for them with exception questions during the session and by recounting these signs in the intervention at the session's end.

As necessary as these questions are, the very ground that underlies them is created from the words and gestures that make up the client's story. In recognizing our clients' need to tell their stories and in acknowledging the healing power that storytelling can have, we also need to respect our clients' abilities as storytellers. They are so good at this at times, and their stories are often so compelling, that it is possible for us to forget the mission that we have as therapists. We forget that our job is to shed light on a dim path for the client; we forego the role of highlighting strength and progress.

To remedy this situation, I have used devices such as note cards containing a drawing similar to the one in figure 8.1, a list of questions that need to be asked in every session, and a personalized format for collecting the needed information. Live supervision is also helpful, though not always available.

Still, I do not always follow the map. When I do meander off the path and become enchanted with parts of the client's story, I lose possible tracks that lead to solutions. If I realize that this is happening, I am gentle with myself. Later, outside the session, I review the part that was so interesting to me and ask myself what was so attractive about it. The client's process is the issue here; my sense is that leaving the path says more about me than it does about the client. My commitment is to take care of my personal issues on my own time and elsewhere.

Case Presentation Format

I have found it useful to talk about cases in professional settings in a format that fits my understanding of the solution-focused model of therapy. In staff meetings where clients are discussed, this format helps to keep the discussion focused on client goals and strengths—and that focus keeps the therapist and other staff concentrated on progress in therapy and what is left to be done to reach client goals.

A presentation using the format on the next page normally takes less than three minutes to complete. Rather than use the term "exceptions," I generally use terms more recognizable to other staff who do not use or may not like this model of therapy. For example, I may simply say, "He overcomes drinking by reading, sleeping, attending an occasional AA meeting, and running out of money." When there are few exceptions, I call our progress "slow." When we have a lot of progress, I am cautious about announcing it. I detail client strategies that work.

Using this format helps staff to concentrate on the client's progress and to give credit to the client for any success. It also eliminates "sightseeing" by staff members who are fascinated by the details of someone else's private life. Even though clients

Case Presentation Format

Client intitals	Date	Session number	Session type

Goal for therapy _____

_____

Client view (list four) _____

_____

_____

Client strengths (list three) _____

_____

_____

Exceptions (list type and number) _____

_____

_____

Task (from exceptions) _____

_____

_____

_____

Client strategies that are working _____

_____

_____

_____

Remaining work to do_____

_____

_____

_____

Staff suggestions _____

_____

_____

_____

are not usually present in staff meetings, my own feeling is that they also benefit when their therapists take the positive approach of offering a discussion based on client strengths. In this way, honoring the client extends from the therapy session throughout the therapist's professional environment.

Discussions with Colleagues

I consider myself very fortunate to have colleagues with other kinds of training besides the solution-focused approach. When discussing cases with colleagues whose ideas differ from mine, I do several things that facilitate the dialogue.

1. I pay close attention to how others word their conclusions about their clients.

2. In most cases, I choose to visit in the world of ideas other than my own, and so I often use their terms when I talk to them.

3. While I still hold to my ideas of client progress, I listen carefully to others' suggestions.

4. I remind myself that my way of working is *not* the only exciting way to work.

5. Any credit for progress goes to the client.

6. I honor the views of my colleagues by refusing to try to convince them to work in the same way I do.

These ideas help me to be realistic about therapy work and my role in that work. I am able to see the value of other therapy models and the work colleagues do. I see the hard work clients do in their situations and recognize the credit belongs to them.

When I hear very different views from my own, I let my internal coach ask me: "What can I learn from this person and this point of view?" If I feel myself becoming irritated or impatient with the person or his or her point of view, I pull my chair up closer to the situation and ask myself, "What is the lesson I need to learn here?"

Essentially, I think of this process as an attempt to apply solution-focused thinking not only to myself and my clients as we work together, but also to myself and my colleagues as we learn from each other. The lessons that I have learned from these kinds of dialogue have been among the most powerful and important in my development as a therapist and, I hope, as a human being. If I choose to look at my own response, I find what I need to correct in my own thinking, and the way I live life or do therapy is enhanced. I realize I do not have to change viewpoints; I can listen and study my own reactions and grow. In so doing, I honor my own efforts and the efforts of my clients and other colleagues. We are all partners in the work of therapy.

9

Strength Undefeatable:
Scaling Questions

To keep our faces toward change and behave like free spirits in the
presence of fate is strength undefeatable.

Helen Keller

Our task is to face fate, face change, and find our undefeatable strength.

When things start to go well in Solution-Focused Therapy, this progress usually happens fairly early on; its appearance is often a surprise to both the therapist and the client. When the therapist offers an affirming atmosphere and searches diligently for client strength, a source of vitality or wisdom is tapped, and the client begins to draw on that source of inner strength.

This is a very different experience from one in which the therapist is described as "empowering" the client. Therapy trainees often use this word; they say that they want to "empower" others. While this sounds like a noble and well-intentioned ambition, in my experience it is neither a practical nor a desirable goal. I have found that the usual outcome is that the therapist's most heroic efforts in this cause are effectively blocked by all the force and ingenuity that the awakened giant of resistance can muster. What else could be expected? "Empowerment" is the therapist's agenda, not necessarily the client's goal.

When trainees talk about empowering others, my internal response is that this wish may well be a projection of their own needs. My question then is, Whose healing work is it that needs more attention? Who is the client here?

When the door to the therapy room closes, the door on our own needs must also close. The next hour belongs to the person in front of me, and the best I can do is be willing to set myself aside, ask the right questions, and expect a change to occur. I can hope for that change and wait patiently for its arrival, and, when it comes, appreciate it in a way that shows the client that it has been recognized.

The only useful strength comes from within the client. It comes in his or her own time and in his or her own way. Thankfully, along each client's path, strength glows even in darkest moments.

Scaling Improvement

This chapter outlines a set of techniques for highlighting client strength as it emerges in therapy. These techniques are called *scaling questions* (Berg 1989).

Scaling questions offer the client and the therapist an opportunity to translate the client's problem and progress toward the stated goal into a single numerical scale that allows both to be evaluated. Numbers on the scale reflect behaviors that have helped a little bit or kept the client going in hard times or helped the client reach success; in this way, from the first session on, any strength that the client shows can be marked in such a way as to make it difficult for the client to forget. Scaling questions help clients set realistic expectations and aim for what is reasonable to expect from themselves and others. Such questions quantify progress and work left to do, highlight coping skills, and help to outline the next steps. They also help the therapist and the client to know when the therapy is finished.

The most powerful application of scaling questions occurs when there has been improvement and the client readily acknowledges this by assigning a number to the extent of the improvement. In doing so, the client is actually complimenting his or her own work—and thereby experiencing a sense of real empowerment and self-confidence.

Scaling questions also address the pace of client progress. Just as we use the client's own language to describe the problem, it is also useful to respect the client's pace. In the design of scaling questions, the language used to describe the problem and the scale used to measure the pace of change are both directed by the client. Accordingly, both elements vary from client to client and often from session to session for each client.

Scaling questions are used to note improvement whenever it occurs—before the first session, during a session, in between sessions, before and after relapse, when things are going well, and near or at the end of therapy. In addition to marking improvements, assessing work left to do, and evaluating recovery from relapse, these questions can be used to measure the client's hope for change, motivation for change, belief that things can change, or willingness to change. The therapist chooses to ask a question about the client's hope or belief or willingness based on the way the client discusses the problem.

The basic wording of any scaling question is as follows: "On a scale of one to ten, with ten being high and one being low, where would you put yourself in your ability to . . . ?"

A form of this question can be woven in at the end of several minutes of exception questions and answers, with the actual content being measured varying according to the client's problem and the details of his or her situation. A scaling question can focus on any movement, no matter how small, toward the client goal. Some clients respond by saying: "Today, I am at a three." And while that may not sound like much progress on a one-to-ten scale, to the client a "three" may mean an enormous move from where he or she has been.

Scaling Improvement Before Therapy Begins

Even in the first session, exception questions can bring to light something useful that the client is doing on her or his own behalf. This is particularly true if the client produces a long list of deliberate exceptions. It is often useful to ask a scaling question that measures progress before the first session and at the end of the first session. In the course of just that single session, the client may move up the scale.

Case Note

"I was at my wit's end"

Therapist: At the time you set the appointment for therapy, where would you put yourself on a scale from one to ten as far as your willingness to work on this problem?

Theo: When I called I was at my wit's end, so maybe a zero.

Therapist: Where would you put yourself now on that same scale?

Theo: A three.

Therapist: What did you do to move yourself up on that scale? *(Honoring movement and beginning to search for exceptions)*

It is often the case that deciding to come for help and making the appointment affect the problem situation in a positive and hopeful way. Any action that clients take in their own behalf usually causes at least a slight improvement. Seeing some improvement at the beginning also gives many clients enough hope to keep trying. Success in any degree is also just a good place to start the search for exceptions.

Scaling Questions During Therapy

During therapy, scaling questions also ask the client to assess his or her progress in the immediate past.

Case Note

"It was harder yesterday"

Therapist: On a scale of one to ten, with ten being high and one being low, where would you put yourself in your ability to overcome the urge to drink today?

Cliff: I would say I am a three.

Therapist: Where were you on that same scale yesterday?

Cliff: That's easy—it was harder yesterday. A one or two for yesterday. Some of my old buddies came around yesterday.

Therapist: Did it help you to overcome the urge to drink—to have them around you, I mean?

Cliff: Well, yes and no. Mostly no, I guess. I wanted to do what we always did; they're still doing it and doing all right.

Therapist: How did you overcome the urge to drink yesterday?

This client's scaled responses offer two possible paths to explore for strength. The first is to explore how this client has managed to move to a "three," from the "one or two" of the day before. This path could be taken in this way:

Therapist: How do you explain that you are at a three today, when yesterday you were at a one or a two?

Cliff: Well, I don't know really, except that my friends aren't around today. They left.

Therapist: Really? Did this help?

Cliff: Well, sort of—it's easier for me not to drink when they aren't around.

Therapist: How did you manage to get them to leave? *(Searching for strength)*

Cliff: I don't think I did it. They did—they just left when I would not drink. *(Although it sounds spontaneous, this may be a deliberate exception)*

Therapist: Did you have an urge to drink when they were there?

Cliff: Sure, wouldn't you? We've been together fifteen years, doing the same stuff all the time. Really, I miss them.

Therapist: Of course, they *are* friends. What did you do to overcome the urge to drink with them this time? *(Accepting the client's view and searching for actions that are exceptions)*

Cliff: I just know I can't do it anymore. I'm killing myself. Slowly, but still killing myself.

Therapist: How did you come up with that idea? *(Searching for cognitive exceptions)*

Cliff: I just told myself that they were dying too and that they looked worse than me. I don't know.

Therapist: How did that help you?

Cliff: I'm not exactly sure. I just told myself that I could kill myself or not today and so could they. I'm the only one who could change this whole thing for me.

Therapist: So, saying this to yourself helped, and reminding yourself that you were killing yourself helped somehow. Was there anything else that helped at this time, even if it helped just a little bit?

Cliff: Well . . . I sort of saw my two kids' faces in their faces. That's kind of weird.

Therapist: How did that help?

Cliff: It made me think that my two kids don't need a drunk daddy anymore.

Therapist: What difference did that make to help you get over the urge to drink this time?

Cliff: I think my kids are tired of a drunk daddy. I can see it in their faces.

Therapist: What difference does that make?

Cliff: It will be their first time to see a real daddy. I want to do that.

Through exploring the client's answer to the original scaling question, a number of exceptions arise. The therapist here is an eager listener; the questions she chooses ask the client to tell her how strong he is at this moment. In responding, the client discovers for himself the basic steps that our Twelve-Step friends suggest are the best medicine for someone newly sober: changing friends, seeing how drinking affects his family, and realizing who is responsible for stopping it. The questions also help him to get in touch with how he found the inner strength to stop himself in one incident.

Questions like these have a perturbing effect; once they are asked, it is difficult for the client to walk away from them. They lead to client strength, and they do so at the client's pace. If a therapist tries to direct a client to take steps like these, the task becomes a much harder one: the client has to be persuaded to "buy" the therapist's ideas and adjust to the therapist's pace and agenda. The client's words are precious to him or her, and the same is true for each client's individual pace.

The second path that the therapist could follow with this same client is to explore how the client avoided slipping back from the previous day's rating.

> *Therapist:* Since you know you were at one or two, yesterday, how do you account for staying above a one and not going all the way to zero? *(Focusing on client strength in any amount)*

> *Cliff:* I only wanted to drink a little bit more than I did today.

> *Therapist:* Is that so? What's the difference?

> *Cliff:* I don't know. I guess I felt a little better yesterday than I did when I was in the hospital. That was the worst time.

> *Therapist:* What made yesterday better than the time in the hospital?

> *Cliff:* I didn't want to drink as much.

> *Therapist:* Is this a little bit different for you?

> *Cliff:* Yes, but not much.

> *Therapist:* How did you arrange to make that difference in your feelings? *(Searching for feeling exceptions)*

> *Cliff:* I guess I decided that I didn't like how I felt in the hospital. So, as bad as things were, I just felt I couldn't start all over again. *(Deliberate feeling exception)*

> *Therapist:* As bad as things were, you got through them anyway. I want to know more about how you did that. What else can you tell me?

> *Cliff:* Not much, except that I got that old taste in my mouth and that made me think how sick I got. *(Another feeling, associated with a sensory memory—a spontaneous exception)*

> *Therapist:* And this helped?

> *Cliff:* I think so. I started to feel sick again.

> *Therapist:* What did you do with it that helped?

The Client's Response

Questioned either way, Cliff may or may not recognize his own wisdom. Often clients give themselves the very answers they seem to need, and yet they do not hear them. The therapy team hears them, and the therapist hears them, but, for whatever reason, the client does not. It is important for the therapist to match the client's mood: if the client is unsure, then the therapist is unsure. There is no dishonesty in this tactic, so long as the therapist has let go of the belief that he or she already knows the client's answers.

If the therapist does mirror the client's doubts, then the therapist's uncertainty makes the client a teacher: the client's new role is to help an eager-to-learn therapist find out exactly which things have improved and understand how they got that way. An intervention is written that sends the client out to study himself or herself and to make a report to the therapist in the next session. This same approach can be taken many times in the course of therapy.

It is also quite often the case that clients are surprised to hear their own answers as they are saying them. The client experiences an "AH-HA!" in mid-sentence and comes up with an answer that he or she didn't know was there. Again, the therapist's job is to continue to respect the client's view and match the client's mood. I usually offer an affirmative response like "Yes, you did, didn't you!"

Case Note

"That's it!"

Therapist: So what was it that helped you move up from a three to an eight this week?

Lisa: I got him to sit down at a time that was good for him and asked him to help me on Saturdays.

Therapist: That's—

Lisa: That's it! The time was good for him. *(Pointing to therapist)* You gave me the answer!

Therapist: I see.

I chose not to argue with this client about who gave her the answer, since accepting her view without judgment allowed her to experience the joy of the moment that she plainly felt.

Similarly, I make no assumptions about the size of a jump a client has made on the scale, either backwards or forwards. The point isn't to force the client's life to conform to some ideal numerical scale; rather, the goal here is to continue to let the client define the amount of progress or relapse and use this self-evaluation to identify the next steps. The numbers are only useful as they are translated into relevant, tried-and-true behaviors that really work.

Scaling Progress and Measuring Success

Scaling questions can be used to mark progress or recovery from a relapse at any point during therapy. Their most powerful use is probably when clients note progress and use the scale to compliment and appreciate their own strength.

Case Note

"Today, at a seven"

Therapist: So, on that same scale, where would you put yourself today in the way you are able to control angry outbursts?

Client: Today, at a seven.

Therapist: What was it that you did that moved you all the way to a seven?

Client: Well, I told you that I've been holding my breath a lot before I speak. I count to ten, sometimes twenty, and tell myself to wait to hear everything the other person is saying.

Therapist: What do you think about moving up to a seven?

Client: I am surprised that I did it. I just hope I can keep it up.

This client brings up a very good point: How will she maintain this level of progress? Another equally important question to ask is whether a "seven" is the number that signifies success for her in this area. Does she need to go higher on the scale? How much work is there left to do?

Therapist: Is seven where you would like to be on average?

Client: I don't know what you mean.

Therapist: Let's say you are successful on a daily basis with controlling your angry outbursts. What number do you think you should reach?

Client: Oh, I see. About eight.

Therapist: And you are at seven right now. What is it going to take to get to eight?

Client: I need to hold my tongue and hold my breath, count to ten when I need to, and make sure I know what the other person means to say before I go nuts on them.

Therapist: Yes, and what will it take for you to do that?

Client: I don't know. I don't think I have ever done it.

Therapist: When was the last time you got close to knowing what the other person meant to say before you went nuts on them? *(Using client words and searching for exceptions)*

Client: Never done it. Not sure I can either.

Therapist: On that scale, how hopeful are you that you could try this, if you really wanted to?

Client: About a ten, if I really wanted to.

The therapist can continue by pressing the client a bit more to think of additional exceptions; if no deliberate ones are found, she can be assigned the task of studying herself to look for times when she gets closer to an "eight" and to notice what she did to get there. She can also be asked to watch herself to see if there are times when she does wait to understand others before she "goes nuts on them." When she reaches an "eight," she may be done with therapy.

Therapist: How long has it been that you have been at an eight?

Client: About three weeks.

Therapist: How much farther do you have to go?

Client: What do you mean?

Therapist: What is left to do?

Client: I need to be at eight most of the time, like I have been.

Therapist: What did it take to stay there?

Client: Just doing what I have done, you know.

Therapist: Of all the things you came up with, what really helped?

Client: Counting to ten and waiting to know what others meant.

Therapist: Is this what keeps it an eight most of the time?

Client: Yes, I think I am about finished on this now.

Scaling Relapse and Recovery

When clients notice that they are in relapse, that realization can be taken as a positive sign: they may already be far enough removed from the relapse to begin finding their way back to the road to recovery. To that end, scaling questions are very versatile. Just as they can be used to measure the progress that clients have made toward the stated therapy goal, they can also be used to assess hope for change in apparently hopeless situations.

Any progress on the scale can be enough to spark the needed change. Even a response of "zero" can be used this way. At least a "zero" isn't a negative number, and clients can be encouraged to see "zero" as a step above "completely falling apart" when compared to a "minus two" or a "minus thirty-five."

Case Notes

"I don't know what happened"

Therapist: So, you went back to a three this week?

Client (exasperated): I don't know what happened.

Therapist: How come it's not at two or even worse?

Client: What do you mean? Isn't three bad enough?

Therapist: Yes, but it could be worse. What did you do to keep control of your angry outbursts at three?

Client: I still held my breath before I spoke and counted to ten. That's it. That is all.

Therapist: What do you think you will have to do to move it to a three and a half or a four?

Client: It should be at a ten.

Therapist: Really? What is reasonable to expect of yourself on the average? (*Using scaling question to set a reasonable goal*)

Client: Probably an eight, like I said.

Therapist: What is the first step you need to take to move back toward an eight?

Client: Do the stuff that works. I mean, do all of it. Can't just do some of it. That's when I slip.

Here, judgment of the client's relapse is suspended; relapse is simply seen as a curve in the road. That point of view helps the client see the road behind and ahead: to refocus on previous progress and return to the work that still needs to be done.

Zona. *In response to a question about her school attendance before coming to therapy, Zona indicated that she had missed four days of school in a row in the previous week. Rather than focus on those four lost days, I asked her how she had managed to make it to school on the one day that she did attend. I remained adamant in my need to understand what made that day different, and the session took off from that direction.*

Therapist: So how did you make it to school on Friday?

Zona: It rained the other days, and I don't like rain. *(Spontaneous exception)*

Therapist: What else made the difference on Friday?

Zona: Nobody bugged me to get out of bed.

Therapist: Is that different?

Zona: Yes, and it will probably never happen again. I live with crazy people.

Therapist: Well, since you live with crazy people, how much hope do you have that you could do it again if you wanted to—let's say on a scale of one to ten? *(Accepting the client view and scaling hope for change)*

Zona: A nine, if I wanted to.

Therapist: What would it take for you to want to do it again? *(Staying with the goal for therapy)*

Zona: Everyone in the house would have to leave me alone—in the morning, I mean.

Therapist: For that to happen, what would you have to do differently?

Zona: I guess I'd have to ask them nicely.

Therapist: How much chance is there of that? *(Flowing with client view and scaling chance for change)*

Zona: Only a little right now.

Therapist: On that same scale, how much chance is there?

Zona: About a six or a seven.

Therapist: What number does it need to be at in order for you to ask them nicely?

Zona: At least an eight.

Therapist: What would it take to move it to an eight?

Zona: I need to talk myself out of being mad.

Therapist: The last time you did this, what helped? *(Exception question)*

Zona: Getting off by myself and thinking till I am tired of thinking about it. *(Deliberate exception)*

Therapist: How did that help? *(Marking client strength)*

Zona: I made up my mind what was best for me.

When Zona came in the next week, she had talked herself into convincing the "crazy people" in her house to let her get up for school on her own, and she had made it to school four out of five days. In effect, we had begun to use the number of days that she attended school as our scale to measure her success.

> *Therapist:* So, you made it to school four out of five days. I am curious about how you did that. *(Searching for exceptions)*

> *Zona:* It was easy. I set the alarm, and got plenty of sleep. I think I need more sleep than other people.

> *Therapist:* How do you know that?

> *Zona:* The more I sleep, the easier it is to get up in the morning.

> *Therapist:* How did you arrange for more sleep then? *(Searching for deliberate exceptions)*

> *Zona:* I just figured out when I was tired and told all of them I was going to bed.

> *Therapist:* So sleep is important to get you up to go to school. What else did you do that helped? *(Searching for more deliberate exceptions)*

> *Zona:* I ignored my brother. He said I was a loser, but I just ignored him and told myself I could do it.

In the next week, Zona attended school all five days, and questions brought out a list of five deliberate exceptions that had enabled her to get there. Moreover, she exhibited a new level of confidence about solving her attendance problems. Shortly before her therapy terminated, after weeks of successfully attending school, Zona slipped back to a week when she attended for only three days.

> *Therapist:* I hear that you made it to school three days this week. Was school closed the other two days?

> *Zona (laughing):* No, no. I just decided I needed a break.

> *Therapist:* I see. Did your break help? *(Accepting client view)*

> *Zona:* Nope. I got in lots of trouble. The crazy people went crazy on me again. Now they think I'll skip some more.

> *Therapist:* Are they right?

> *Zona:* No, they are not right. They still think I am a baby, and that's not true.

> *Therapist:* Oh? How do you know that?

> *Zona:* Because I can do what I need to do to take care of myself.

> *Therapist:* Really? And what is that?

> *Zona:* Look, all it takes is to set my alarm, tell myself I have to be there or there will be all kinds of trouble at home, and go to bed on time.

The confident tone in Zona's voice was a clear sign that she knew what she needed to do to recover from her relapse. I finished this sequence by scaling her certainty that she could change to avoid the "trouble at home" and exploring times when she has been able to do so.

Supporting Client Success

Continued progress leads to a stage known as the "success sequence"; this is a time in therapy when the goal has been achieved and clients seem to be holding steady with their improvements. This stage can frighten clients who are unused to success or fearful that the gains they have made will not last. Beginning therapists also often tend to doubt that the improvement is real; instead of supporting the change that has occurred, they may actually negate its potential in the client's life.

Scaling questions help to keep these doubts in perspective by continuing to define the progress that has been made and any unfinished work that the client identifies. They also help by making sure that the goal the client has set is a realistic one. For example, when a client states that she wants to stay at a "nine" in overcoming her urge to nag, I first ask if this is a realistic goal as an average. If she feels that it is (and I rely on the client's judgment to make that decision), we go on to explore what it will take to stay at a "nine." We do so by reviewing the client strengths (in the form of deliberate exceptions) that move the client's coping ability up the scale and keep it there.

Case Note

"I'm not sure about a nine." Caren had given herself the goal of reaching a nine in overcoming her urge to nag her husband, and she had been making steady progress for some time.

Therapist: Things have been going rather well for a while now. Are you still at a nine?

Caren: Yes, I've been at a nine for the last two weeks.

Therapist: What are you doing to maintain a nine?

Caren: It seems to me that I do the same things each time, and as long as they work I'll keep doing them.

Therapist: What are these things that work for you?

Caren: Well, first, I guess, I hold my breath, and usually count to ten. Before I reach five, I start telling myself that I can have my opinion and don't really need to force it on him.

Therapist: How does this help?

Caren: Sometimes I hear myself in my head, and I know I sound like my mom, in the way she used to yell at my dad. I know I didn't like that, and I know my kids don't like it either.

Therapist: How does remembering this help?

Caren: I stop myself if I have to when I know what I sound like.

Therapist: What else helps?

Caren: If I say the Serenity Prayer.

Therapist: What do you think you will have to do to keep this going at a nine?

Caren: The main thing for me is I've got to stop myself.

Therapist: What is the most useful thing you have found to stop yourself?

Caren: I've got to listen to myself more often and try that prayer.

Therapist: What is realistic as an average on the scale from one to ten?

Caren: It is probably around a seven and a half or an eight. I'm not sure about a nine, but maybe I can stay at a nine.

In the next week, Caren "slipped" back to an eight and was distraught about the slip. I offered the the consoling thought that problems sometimes get worse before they get better, and together we explored what was realistic for her to expect of herself on a regular basis. She decided that an eight was probably good enough, but that she wanted to be at a nine. We reviewed what she had done to keep herself from going lower than an eight and went on to explore what success would mean for her when therapy was over. At what number would she find herself? What would it take to get her there? By the end of the session, she had decided that eight was a good average number to maintain and that reaching it would mean that she had been successful in therapy.

Terminating Therapy

Since scaling questions throughout therapy are used to measure how close the client is to the goal, it is easy for both therapist and client to keep the end in focus—a main goal of Solution-Focused Therapy.

Case Note

"I'm ready to try this on my own"

Therapist: It has been two weeks, and you are saying that you have stayed at an eight or higher.

Caren: I know. Things are going well now.

Therapist: How will you know when to end our time together?

Caren: I need to stay at an eight or more for a little while longer.

Therapist: What will tell you that therapy has been a success for you?

Caren: I can say I'm around an eight, and my husband will be more sure of the change in me.

Therapist: What will it take for him to be more sure of the change?

Caren: He'll have to see me not nag him a few more times.

Therapist: How sure are you that you can keep this going so that he will be more sure?

Caren: I'm doing it now. I'm ready to try this on my own.

I have found that clients often know when therapy is about to finish. I am always glad to hear that my services are no longer needed, since this is a good sign that I have done my job: the client has discovered that life can be lived without a therapist and that he or she can take on the situation without me. Other clients have told me that they "could now do it on their own," that they "would take it the rest of the way," or simply that they "just did not need me anymore." A client can give himself or herself no higher compliment.

In one case, a twelve-year-old girl was referred by her mother for therapy. She had just moved to a new house, started classes at a new junior high school, had her ears pierced, and received new braces. Her mother's concern was that her daughter needed higher self-esteem.

After eight sessions of twenty minutes each, the client informed her therapist that she believed she had gotten all she could out of therapy. She would call for therapy again when *she* felt she needed it. She had achieved her goals: she talked and walked differently and sounded confident, and she reported feeling higher self-esteem. A call to her mother confirmed these changes. The members of our team found it amusing that our therapist and the team had been "let go" by a client who had self-esteem problems. Being fired seemed the best evidence of all that her dilemma was solved.

Scaling Questions for Couples or Families

Moving from therapy with individuals to therapy with couples or family members makes the matrix for healing larger and more complex, but not unmanageable. Whether the couple or group agrees on a single goal for therapy or not, the therapist proceeds by asking relationship-oriented exception questions. Asking scaling questions that are similarly relationship oriented will also help to draw on the strengths of the individuals involved and on the strength of the relationships between them.

Case Note

"I can't give up." An interview with three members of a family of four began with the mother, brother, and father complaining about the absent brother. All agreed that the absent person was "the family problem." Each of the three seemed fascinated by the comings and goings of this fourth member of their family. Each thought him "crazy" and in need of immediate inpatient treatment. An unsuccessful commitment hearing for this brother had led the family to conclude that the state's mental health system "stunk." The therapist accepted their view of their problem and began the process of helping them set a new goal by asking this question to each member present: "Since you feel that the system stinks, and it looks like there is no help in sight, what do you think is reasonable for you to do in your situation?"

> *Mother:* I don't know. See, no one will help us—no matter what we try. I can't give up—he's my son. No good mother gives up on her son. I'll keep trying to get him help.

> *Father:* My hands are tied—there's nothing I can do. It just stinks.

> *Brother:* I think he's selfish. I just don't give a damn no way.

> *Therapist (to each):* What is reasonable for you to expect from yourselves given that he does not seem to be changing?

> *Mother (resolutely):* I will *not* give up.

> *Therapist (to brother and father):* Do you think this is what you will do too—do what Mom is doing?

> *Brother:* No, I'm giving up—it's the only thing I can do.

> *Therapist (to all three):* How will that help you?

Father: Well, I'm for that too, because anything else will drive me crazy.

Therapist (to father): Is Mom's idea a good one for her?

Father: Well, she's like that, you know—she really can't help it.

Therapist (to mother): Are they right? Are there times when you handle this better?

Mother: When I am busy.

Therapist: How does being busy help?

Mother: I don't think or worry as much.

The therapist went on to ask what she did to keep busy, and she offered several deliberate exceptions. In order to scale this for the family, the therapist asked the mother how much better she was when she was busy. She stated that she was at a four on a one-to-ten scale; when not busy, she was at zero. Questions were then put to the father and brother about the times when the mother was handling things better.

Therapist (to father): On that same scale, from one to ten, how much better is Mom when she is busy?

Father: I'd say she is at five or six, when she is busy. She's better when she has something in her life besides her children.

Therapist: Like what?

Brother: Like the dog, her work, visiting her sister, and talking on the damn phone. She's better when she's on the phone to a friend.

Father: But we're all better when we're busy. We need to see that we've done what we can do, and until he gets dangerous we can't really do anything.

Therapist (to father): When he's not busy, where would you put Brother's ability to get along on that same scale from one to ten?

Father: About an eight, when he's busy. He's okay when he's busy. I'm at a six or seven when I'm busy. But he's my son, and it is on me and his mom.

The session continued with questions asking each member of the family to comment on how "being busy" helped each of them and each of the others. The therapist went on to ask how they came up with these helpful ideas. The atmosphere in the therapy room as the family hesitantly began to address its strengths was very touching. Repeatedly, I find that individuals and relationships do have just the strength they need to go one more step. Reaching that next step means finding more strength and more of their own wisdom.

For each person present in a session with a couple or a family, the therapist gathers views, compliments, and exceptions in relation to the stated therapy goal. Working this way with more than one person takes a rigorous commitment on the therapist's part—a commitment to gathering all of the elements needed for an intervention for each person. I have also found that it takes courage to watch a family struggle and refuse to step in to "fix" their problem for them. Patience and trust on the therapist's part can help the session be a place where the clients' inner wisdom emerges from within.

Clients pay close attention to scaling questions no matter how they are used. They start out invested in the discussion of a problem that they considered important enough to involve a professional, and they are even more invested in questions that give them hope or take stock of the improvements they have made. Their focus is further pointed toward change; the air in the therapy room grows expectant, and the language of change assures that the solution is on its way.

10

Worst-Case Scenarios

You are never given a problem without a gift for you in its hands.

Richard Bach

Often gifts are wrapped in odd packages; our job is to
open and receive.

Clients often enter therapy at times when they are "just getting by" or "all hell has broken loose." In either case, they are usually worn to a frazzle and at their wits' end. They see their situations as hopeless and themselves as helpless, or they feel trapped in their current circumstances.

It is crucial for the therapist to accept the client's view of these circumstances, match the client's mood, and visit them in the place where they say they are—while at the same time holding on to the thought that they can know their strength again. Perhaps the therapist's most vital function is to harbor hope for them when they do not see any hope in their situations.

To this end, it is particularly important to gather information in the usual way. The therapist simply accepts the air of hopelessness in the therapy room as being true for now and moves ahead with the usual perturbing questions, listening closely to the client's story and paying careful attention to the client view, client compliments, and any deliberate or spontaneous exceptions.

In this chapter, we look at some specific strategies for those desperate times. Techniques to reawaken each client's inner resources are drawn from the work of experts and from my own experience. That experience leads me to approach each situation with similar expectations: I trust the client to find the way out. And I trust that he or she is already doing just that.

Just Getting By

The first assumption I make is that clients who are "just getting by" have not yet given up on their situation. They are still alive, and they are still coming to therapy; by virtue of these facts, in some measure they are still coping. The therapist's first task is to search for anything else that the client is doing that may be helping even in a small way. That small amount may be all it takes for the needed solution to emerge.

Berg and deShazer (1991) have called the technique used in this context *coping questions* because the questions used here focus on how the client is currently managing to get by in his or her situation. These questions search beyond the client's dismal view of the present to find exceptions in the daily struggle. These questions differ from other exception questions in that they are not aimed at finding times when the problem is different or better; rather, the focus is on what the client is currently doing to cope.

The power of these questions is that they are interventions in themselves. Like exception questions, coping questions need only be asked; the client does not necessarily need to answer them. And, in fact, the usual client response during this kind of session is to remain depressed and disheartened. It is a good idea not to tamper with this mood; the therapist should simply recognize it as valid, given the life circumstances of the client. Yet the questions have the effect of poking holes in the client's mood after the session is over and the client begins to move away from his or her current state toward new thoughts, feelings, or behaviors.

Here are some guidelines for using coping questions.

1. Accept the client view and language.

2. Recognize that change may be slow.

3. Remember that the client is strong and has already done a few things to "get by."

4. Stay focused on the job of finding those things that have helped.

5. Find compliments that the client will believe to be true.

6. Use exception questions aimed at finding out how the client has been coping in spite of the difficult situation he or she is facing.

Questions for individual clients:

• Things are really rough for you right now. What has helped you get through this?

• Are there times when you notice that you are dealing with this a little better?

• How in the world have you gotten through this?

• What do you do that helps even a little bit?

Questions for couples or family members:

• What have you noticed he is doing that helps him get by?

• Are there times when your husband gets along a little bit better? What is he doing differently at that time?

• What would he say you were doing when he was handling this better?

• Is there something that he thinks you do to help him get along a little better?

• What would your wife say you are doing differently when you are getting through each day?

• What helps you feel better when he is not doing so well?

Case Note

"I'll do it if that is what it will take"

Therapist: Things are pretty rough right now. *(To wife)* How have you been able to keep going?

Wife: I don't know. If one more person dies, I'll give up.

Therapist: It is rough to have all this at once. I am real concerned about what is keeping you going. What do you think keeps you going even a little bit? *(Searching for strength)*

Wife (pointing to her husband): He does. If it wasn't for him, I'd just give up. He is stronger.

Therapist (with interest): Really? How does he help you?

Wife: He takes the kids when things get too much for me.

Therapist: How does he know to do that? *(Searching for her strength)*

Wife: He can just tell.

Therapist (to husband): You must know her very well.

Husband: She has a look on her face that says, "I'm going to scream—come help me!"

Therapist: And you know this look, don't you?

Husband: Of course, wouldn't you? I've lived with her look for five years.

Wife: Longer than that. *(Crying)*

Therapist (to husband): What have you noticed she's been doing when she is taking this a little better?

Husband: She's only getting by, you know—but I think when she talks to her sister or goes to see her. This helps for an hour or two. Then she's back to crying.

Therapist: Do you think crying helps her at all?

Husband: Probably, because it's the thing to do when you lose family. It's hard for me to watch.

Therapist (to husband): Sure it is. What else has helped her to hang on these days?

Husband: If she can be alone for a half hour—away from the kids and away from me. She does too much for all of us. Right now she can't really do too much. I have to help.

Therapist (to wife): Does he know what you mean by help?

Wife: Yes, he's done it before.

Therapist (to wife): What did it take to get him to help before? *(Searching for an exception in the behavior that helped the husband to help his wife)*

Wife: He cut down on his work hours.

Therapist (to husband): How did you come up with that idea?

Husband: I thought it would help her, and it did. She came around.

Therapist: Is that possible now?

Husband: We'd be cutting it close—real close.

Therapist: On a scale of one to ten, how willing are you to cut it close if it means helping her at the same time?

Husband: I'll help. About an eight.

Therapist (to wife): Do you believe him?

Wife: Yes, I guess so. He shouldn't have to quit just to help me.

Husband (to wife): I'll do it if that's what it will take.

The rest of this interview was devoted to the husband's understanding of how his wife was making it through her current situation. Often, if a family member who is "just getting by" cannot remember what has helped, I have found that other family members can. In any case, it is crucial to honor all of the client's responses. If nothing that an individual client is doing, thinking, or feeling helps even a little bit, I go on to ask the client what else they have tried or what they have thought about trying.

At times, clients will say, "I don't know what to do." I have responded to these clients in this way: "Yes, that's true. If you did know, what would you be doing differently?" This question opens the door to possible solutions and usually calls forth at least the beginning of a useful response or a stirring of thoughts from clients.

The strength and wisdom of family members should not be overlooked in cases where individuals see little hope in their situation. Trusted to operate on their own, without the therapist's advice, preaching, or hidden agendas, families usually do masterfully well. They make good decisions about who should come for therapy, when they should arrive, and how the problem should be discussed.

I have repeatedly noticed family members acting as the eyes and ears that others in the family need. Where one member feels weak, another will pitch in like clockwork with the exact element needed to secure healing for the family. I have seen family members step out of their usual roles in order to take on the responsibilities that another family member has traditionally held. Children and adults alike take part, just to help the family. This "switching" knows no boundaries; the abilities that some family members are known for arise in others when these are most needed.

As amazing and unexpected as this wisdom can be, I have found one thing to be certain: if I think that I know where the wisdom lies in a family, I am bound to be fooled. I can and do count on that.

It is exciting to notice how family members watch one another. Families do this "watching" to different degrees; when they are adept at it, this watchfulness can add a great strength to their power to hear and to heal.

When individual clients place a high value on the opinions of others, this kind of "dependence" can be seen as a similar resource. Questions like these can lead to new exceptions or useful alternative strategies: "What do your parents *(or friends)* say you should do? Are they right? What else have they told you to try? Are they right?" The point is that wisdom is not locked up in any one person; rather, it grows in power through *relationships*. The same web of connections that produces family conflicts can also be a source of empowerment for the family and each of its members.

And then there are times when the bottom falls out, all hell breaks loose, and the worst seems here to stay.

When All Hell Breaks Loose

These are the clients most therapists dread to see. Their problems have usually lasted for many years. They are often chronic complainers and are rarely "doers." They have a litany of complaints, and in one session the therapist is likely to hear this litany recited several times. Many therapists expect little of these clients and hold even less hope for their situations. They are often viewed as resistant to change, since their progress is usually remarkably slow in comparison to other clients.

In short, before therapy has begun, this kind of therapist's attitude makes it likely that no change will occur. Expectations are minimal to begin with, and the client will take the blame when the therapy goes nowhere—if the therapist does not check these preconceptions at the door. The sole alternative is not one that most of us look forward to. The therapist must simply spend some time in the client's hell in order to honor the client who is in this kind of situation. Isn't this our job?

It is fortunate for the therapist that the therapy hour is just a visit in each client's world. Yet for that hour, we must set ourselves aside and let clients lead us into their world of darkness and pain. Our clients will let us know how their cooperation can be obtained; we need only listen carefully and stay alert for the appearance of anything that lightens that darkness or helps them to hang on and survive the pain.

A set of questions can be used to honor the point of view that the client holds about the problem and look for strength within that point of view. Berg and deShazer (1991) have termed these kinds of questions the *pessimistic sequence*. The term is appropriate, since this approach works with the worst human situations, and clients tend to view these dilemmas with attitudes of hopelessness and discouragement.

Questions for individual clients in worst-case situations:

- Well, you are right—things are worse than ever. Can you imagine things getting even worse? What do you suppose keeps things from getting that bad? How does that help?

- What are you doing that keeps things from getting any worse now? What were you able to do today that kept you going? How did that help?

- Since things are so bad, and nothing can be done, what has kept you from giving up altogether? How does that help?

- Is this the worst that it's ever been? What helped you to get out of bed this morning? What helped you to get to my office? How did that help?

- What do you think keeps you from going to pieces over this? How does that help?

Clients cling to the facts of these situations that "prove" how awful things are. The therapist will be wise to let them have that view and make no attempt to talk them out of it. If persuasion is used, clients will simply dig in their heels and close off any hope for another view. Each question about what the client is doing to get through his or her dilemma is followed by a question asking the client *how* something helped. The therapist's persistence in compiling a list of these "things that helped" and trying to understand how they helped will ensure that a lengthy portion of the session will be spent discussing client strength.

Case Note

"My depression is the worst it has ever been." A student came for therapy with all the symptoms, gestures, and problems that go along with depression. Her tone of voice affirmed her statement that she was more depressed than she had ever been.

Tina: It has never been worse than it is now. I don't want to eat, and I don't like to sleep. *(Moaning)*

Therapist: What time of day is it the very worst?

Tina: Oh, in the morning, for sure.

Privately, I told myself that this admission was a victory: since her depression was at its worst in the morning, by definition it was at least a little better throughout the rest of the day. Such a concession should give us fertile ground to search for deliberate exceptions.

Therapist: So something is better at night?

Tina: Well, a little.

Therapist: What is different at night?

Tina: I am not thinking about stuff that worries me. I am doing things with my friends and studying. . . .

There it was—a possible breakthrough for her in her depression. Of course, we still needed to search for more exceptions and scale her willingness to work on the problem. The interview ended with homework that included six deliberate exceptions and a distinct improvement in her mood. Her sense of depression continued to lift and was gone within three weeks. All this followed from the intervention of three simple questions.

Questions for relationships in worst-case situations:

- The three of you have really been through it this week. Is this the worst that things can get?

- Things sound awful. What keeps you from giving up?

These questions should be directed to each person in the room. If all respond in a similar way, the therapist can explore the situation at its worst and find out what each did to get through it. If one client cannot remember what he or she did or is finding it especially hard to cope, the therapist will do well to accept these as the "expected" responses to stress. The others in the group can be asked to comment on what they have seen the stressed person do to cope, no matter how minimal an effort has been made. Others can often provide helpful details about how a person has managed to get through tough times, and the individual who is struggling is immediately helped by hearing others talk about his or her strength.

- What have you seen your mother do that tells you she is not falling apart completely?

- On a scale of one to ten, with one being low and ten being high, where would you put yourself today in regard to how you are handling this awful situation?

- On that same scale, where would you put your mother's ability to cope?

Clients in these kinds of situations place themselves at zero or below. I have found it helpful to respond by asking:

- How do you account for it being at zero and not at minus ten? What helped? How did that help?

- What do you think your son would say is the reason things are no lower than zero? How do you think that has helped?

- What did you have to do to keep it from getting any lower than it already is? What else has helped?

The questions used should always be fashioned to match the client's situation and mood, using his or her views and language. No matter how bad the situation gets, clients are still married to their opinions and to their own ways of describing the events in their lives. When all else seems lost, at least these expressions remain. The therapist can share the client's awareness for the therapy hour, honor what is going on with the client, and see tremendous changes in a short period of time.

Case Note

"I feel for him because it's hard for me." *A family just beginning the process of recovery from alcohol addiction had been making progress in the areas of maintaining sobriety and improving communication between the parents. The couple came in for therapy following a sudden blowup between them during which the husband had hit his wife. Both said that things were the worst they had ever been. Each partner was extremely argumentative and ready to blame the other.*

Therapist: Is this the worst things have ever been?

Husband: Yeah. I've got to stay sober. She can't take that from me; she's done it before. Then I drink.

Wife: You'll take it from me before I get drunk because of you.

Therapist: Since this is the worst it can be and one of you may get the other drunk *(accepting their views)*, what is it that keeps you together? *(Searching for strength)*

Wife: I know what he is going through, trying to stay sober—it's really hard. I feel for him because it's hard for me. *(The husband nods his head in agreement)*

Therapist: Oh? How does knowing what he's going through help you at this time?

Wife: It makes me stop and think about what I say to him.

Husband: Yeah, she's right. I can stop, too—I just didn't this time. I hit her. *(Sobbing)*

Therapist: Were there times when you hit her before? *(Both nod yes)* Was there any difference this time?

Wife: There was only one hit, and it didn't hurt me like before. When he hit me, we both stopped. That has never happened.

Husband: I got away from her right away.

Therapist: How? What did you do?

Wife: He ran to the bedroom—

Husband (interrupting): And called my sponsor.

Therapist: Is this different? *(Both nod yes)* What else was different about this time?

Wife: I didn't go after him.

Therapist: What did you do instead?

Wife: I walked away, prayed the Serenity Prayer, and read my Big Book.

Therapist: How did this help?

Wife: I got calmed down. I didn't go around him that night.

Therapist (to wife): What did you see him doing that somehow got him through this awful moment? *(A question that asks her to study him)*

Wife: I heard him pick up the phone to call his sponsor.

The interview continued to explore the differences they had noted in each other. In the past, their battles had become screaming matches, ending in long bouts of physical violence. Now the blaming ceased and melted into an understanding of each other's pain. Since each knew how difficult it was to stay sober and face life that way, each also understood the other's challenges. Their strength was obvious to me: they were able to face their problem and the part that each played in it squarely, acknowledging their individual feelings and keeping focused on what each needed to do to stay sober.

These are all issues that individuals new to recovery face—and, in fact, the cornerstones of the first stage of a solid recovery program. Now they were taking the courageous step of facing these issues without the usual anesthesia of their drug of choice. I could only applaud what seemed to be a breakthrough in a long-established pattern.

A solution-focused approach invites therapists to see crises like these as opportunities and to expect to see a chance for change in the most longstanding problems. Maybe it really is darkest before the dawn; in any case, the darker moments offer each of us a chance to wait expectantly for new light.

11

Crises and Urgent Problems

Human beings, by changing the inner attitudes of their minds, can change the outer aspects of their lives.

William James

What we think about anything determines what we do with it.

In any style of therapy, the perception a therapist has of a problem will determine how it is handled and how treatment will progress. Especially in times of urgent crisis, our response to a client's problem is often colored by our own experience. Therapists who have resolved their own personal emergencies well and worked through any residual emotions are likely to listen more carefully and harbor hope for change in the life of the client. Unresolved, unattended, or unidentified personal issues can make it difficult for the therapist to see what the client is seeing. With preconceptions of any kind, the problem as the client sees it can get lost, and therapy can become an act of persuasion.

Yet crises and emergencies call forth human strength. A crisis led a slave trader to suddenly reform and write the popular hymn "Amazing Grace." Another beloved hymn, "It Is Well with My Soul," was written by a man who had just lost his family on the high seas. His decision to view horror in a different way than most people is an emblem of what people can do in the face of the worst of human situations.

So it is with therapy. How the therapist characterizes a situation can serve as a compass for a whole new direction in the client's life. The evaluation made and the method of therapy chosen can offer the client hope—or defer a chance to make real change. If the therapist's expectations are low—whether based on research, similar cases, personal experience, or fear—then the client may be closed off from the vitality hope offers.

In my own work, I have found it useful to wait for the client's reaction to any situation; I study that reaction carefully and let it guide my own response. I refuse to push; I acknowledge the client's view and know that in time it will change.

As therapists, then, we can choose how we look at urgent and chronic problems. If we suspend interest in any particular outcome for each and every client, then a universe of outcomes is possible—and hope is always among the possibilities.

This chapter addresses suicide, addiction issues, and child abuse. Interview formats and guidelines for use of these formats are offered. In each case, the choice has been made to view all of these human dilemmas with the expectation that strength will emerge in the face of every adversity.

Basic Guidelines for Urgent Situations

1. Take responsibility for your own view of the problem. If your view is not a hopeful one, be willing to examine the effects of your attitude on the therapy.

2. Accept the client view as true for her or him. See the world as the client sees it.

3. Use the client's language. Honor the meaning the client places on his or her words. Ask the client to clarify his or her meaning if it seems confusing or unclear.

4. Ask each client to pick a specific goal.

5. Listen for strength. Use worst-case-scenario questions to elicit strength. Ask about the likelihood of the client using strategies that have worked in the past. Be persistent in fully exploring any strength that the client shows.

6. Offer an intervention that uses the client view, client compliments, and any strength that is evident.

7. Schedule the next session within a few days. Make contingency plans and use them if they are needed.

Suicide

This section is really a gift from a client who faced the crisis of suicide. Previously I had found counseling suicidal clients exhausting and inconclusive work. A high school student taught me to think about the problem in a very different way.

Case Note

"You ask a lot of dumb questions. Did you know that?" I met this client when she entered the teachers' lunchroom where I was eating with her school counselor. We were discussing the counselor's caseload of 900 students when a young woman plopped herself down in front of us and announced, "Tomorrow, I will be dead!" Her counselor and I looked at each other; clearly our caseload discussion would have to be suspended for a time.

I listened to Pam tell the story of a girl who lost her childhood before it began. She had taken care of her addicted parents, lived in numerous foster homes, and been in trouble with the law. She had failed in school the previous year. She hated the group home where she lived and the judge who would soon decide her next move. "I give up! There's nothing else to live for!"

Her description of each of these experiences was vehement and emotional. Each situation had worsened her life. As I listened, my respect grew for this girl who had lived through all these things and survived. She had given much thought to her decision to end her life. She knew when and how her death would occur. She chose to make her decision known, rather than simply let her body be discovered after the act.

Here is an excerpt from that interview, a gift she gave to me that day.

Pam: I am going to die.

Therapist: Oh?

Pam: Yes, tomorrow you will find me. . . .

Therapist: What brought all this on?

Pam: Well, just how would you like to have a drunk for a father? Not know where your mother is? Have to run away to get anywhere? *(Sobbing)*

The story she told for the next ten minutes was an uninterrupted chain of misery. Here was a person who had faced more human heartache in sixteen years than most people face in a lifetime. I carefully noted the words she used to portray her problem. I remembered the questions to use for worst-case scenarios and waited for her to take a breath. When she finally did pause to inhale, I asked:

Therapist: This is one of the worst situations I've ever heard. Since everything is *so* rotten, how do you explain that you were able to get out of bed this morning?

Pam (looking stunned and stumbling over her words): I had band practice at three today. . . .

Therapist (unconvinced): So? What does that have to do with anything? *(Looking for a sign of strength)*

Pam: Well, I'm good in band—not all that good, but better than some. Anyway, I have to go to it because I'm a majorette and the group depends on me.

Therapist (puzzled): What difference does that make? I mean, given that everything is awful—

Pam (interrupting): Because I'm not going to be like my dad—he's an old drunk and good for nothing!

Therapist (more puzzled): And you want to be different from him?

Pam: Yeah. His life is a mess. So's mine. I don't like living at this home.

Therapist: What else helped you to get to school today?

Pam (stunned again): I had a math test at eleven. I got a B.

Therapist (mystified): What difference did that make? I mean, given how bad it all is—

Pam: I told you—I ain't gonna be like my dad. He never finished school. I probably won't either—I failed last year, you know.

Therapist: I see. How are you doing this year?

Pam: B-minus average. Not very good, huh?

Therapist (in an unbelieving tone): Really? How did you do that? I mean, from an F the year before . . . I don't understand.

Pam spent the next few minutes helping me to believe that she really had brought her grades up from an F to a B minus. She related many things she had done to make this happen. Her new grade average had permitted her to take part in band. She had missed going to Japan with the band the previous year.

Therapist: What else helped you to get out of bed this morning?

Pam: See, I got this meeting at the house this afternoon to settle the new girls' problems.

Therapist (unbelieving): So how did that help?

Pam (disgusted that she has to keep explaining things to the therapist): Look, they're new. They need help, like I did when I first got there. Now I'm the oldest resident, and they look up to me to help them solve problems.

Therapist: What does that mean to you?

Pam: I'm tired of it right now, but I like it because I can help them. You ask a lot of dumb questions—did you know that?

Therapist (with a sigh of agreement): Yes, I know my questions are dumb. It's too bad I don't know any others. *(Matching her view)*

Pam: They're college questions, aren't they? Is that where you learned them?

Therapist: Well, yes.

Pam (softly): I want to go to college.

School counselor: And you could, if you want.

Pam (looking at therapist): You know what I want to be, don't you? A counselor. But I have too many problems, and counselors don't have ones like I have.

Therapist: I'm not so sure. Some of the best counselors have had a lot of hard problems. There could be a way.... *(Matching her degree of hope)*

The conversation veered off into possible college plans and then on to a specific plan for the next few hours. She wouldn't kill herself; she and her counselor reached an agreement to that effect. This agreement was enhanced by their plans to see each other at the football game that night, and by Pam saying that she felt better—good enough to go back to class, band practice, and the meeting at the group home that afternoon. She also promised to let her counselor know if she needed any help that afternoon.

She got up to leave; she hugged her counselor and shook her head at me. Over her shoulder, she threw this in my direction: "You're really weird."

Now, what happened here? First, I suspended my own fears of death and suicide and instead simply visited her in her world. I had no doubt that her world was awful, and I believed and affirmed her view that it was. At the same time, I asked some of the troubling questions designed for worst-case scenarios. In doing so, I chose to avoid showing any fascination with her interest in dying. Her response was to argue for life.

In other suicide incidents, I had tried to argue for life—and my clients had argued for death. These interviews had been completely draining and seemed to resolve nothing. After hours of effort, I still did not know if my client would be alive the next day. Even with the best contingency plans, I still feared for their lives.

I felt I had been given a strange gift, wrapped in a most threatening package: an idea for a format for a suicide interview. I had been searching for such a format for some time: a brief and comprehensive format that reflected the known research on suicide and would work with any client who viewed death as an option.

The tool that resulted has since been used successfully by many clinicians in their work. The form can be adapted or used exactly as it is, with the therapist filling in the form as each of its questions are asked. The completed form may then be added as is to the client or patient record.

The first part of this interview format covers the usual information gathered in a suicidal situation. The next part covers the frequency of thoughts about suicide and the coming and going of these thoughts—how long the thoughts stay and what the client is doing to make them go away. These questions begin exploring how the client has survived up to this point and what is keeping them from ending it all now. A number of exception questions include what deShazer and Berg (1988) call a *miracle question*, a question asked in the hope of finding a reasonable goal still worth the effort in the client's life.

The client's shift from a person who welcomes death to an individual facing life again is often quick. I have been surprised and grateful to see this turn occur time and time again in a variety of settings.

Addictions

Much of my work has been done with persons who are addicted to something, whether alcohol, drugs, work, spending, food, sex, approval, or some other form of dependence. In each case, I have found it helpful to set aside my own assumptions about recovery and focus on working with the individual client. I do keep in mind current information on addiction issues, including ideas drawn from Twelve-Step programs and elsewhere about what people often face as they recover; yet I am careful not to let these ideas prevent me from seeing each client as a teacher in his or her own right. The client is the expert, and I am there to learn about the reality of recovery from the person actually going through the process.

Whether working with individuals, couples, groups, or families, it is useful to know how long each client had been addicted, what stage in the recovery process the client has reached when therapy begins, who else is affected by the client's addiction, and its effects on the whole person—the physical, emotional, mental, and spiritual dimensions of the client's life. It is crucial to accept recovering clients just as they are, with no attempt to correct and thereby enable or disable them further. I discipline myself with private self-talk about the limits of my role, so that my own recovery issues stay shelved during the course of therapy for my clients.

A number of the case notes presented in earlier chapters have dealt with clients in recovery. Therapists counseling clients struggling with alcoholism or other addictions will find that solution-focused guidelines are particularly valuable in helping clients set reasonable therapy goals. These guidelines also help the therapist to appreciate the manner in which each client has achieved sobriety. A solution-focused approach helps therapists to respect the client's current stage in recovery, honor client feelings and thoughts, and support each individual journey through the recovery process.

The two cases presented here focus on the special problems of counseling clients new to recovery and on the impact that addictions have on others, especially family.

Case Note

"We think we are approaching normal, whatever that is." A married couple in their early forties were referred to therapy by their doctor, our unit's addictions specialist. At the time of the first appointment, both had been sober for an entire week for the first time in nearly twenty years. He had become sober in AA, and she had completed a 28-day treatment program; both came to therapy with the primary goal of maintaining sobriety and also to work

Guide for a Suicide Interview

This interview format is offered as a help to counselors who work with persons talking about dying and suicide. The interview uses a solution-focused approach and takes about 30 to 45 minutes to complete.

1. Since the client is in front of you, he or she is still very much alive. By talking about death, the client is giving a cry for help.

2. Remind yourself that there is hope for survival. Your job is to find a way to spotlight and capitalize on the hope that is there.

3. Document the interview and your actions on this form.

Client _____Age _____Gender _____

Referred by _____Date _____

How client sees the problem _____

_____

_____

Available support systems _____

_____

Typical symptoms _____

_____

Does client have a plan for his or her own death? _____

Date _____Time _____Method _____

Previous attempts? _____

Current medications _____Taken as prescribed? _____

Current drug use _____Taken/not taken? _____

Frequency of thoughts of dying or suicide _____

How long do these thoughts last? _____

What happens to these thoughts? _____

When thoughts are reduced or go away, what is the client doing to make that happen? _____
_____

If a miracle occurred and the problem was solved, what would the client be doing differently? _____
_____

What is the client doing to make this situation a little bit better? _____
_____

What else has the client thought, felt, or done to help him or her get through the day? _____
_____

What helped the client to get to this session? _____
_____

On a scale of one to ten, how likely is it that the client will continue to do these things that have helped?_____

Which parents or relatives have been contacted? _____

What was their response? _____

Who else has been contacted? _____

What was their response? _____

Suggestions from colleagues _____
_____

Recommendations _____
_____

Counselor's signature _____Date _____

on "anything else that comes up." When they arrived for the first session, their six-year-old son was with them; he made the announcement that began the interview.

Tim: We are all sober this week!

Therapist: Really! Is that different?

All (nodding): Yes.

Father: Sure is a different world.

Mother: Yes, for all of us.

Therapist: What did you all do to make that happen?

Father: Read the Big Book, talked to my sponsor, went to meetings.

Mother: Yes, he's been to a meeting every day in the last week.

Therapist: Do you think that is what helped?

Mother: I think so. It helps me too that he goes.

Therapist: Well, that's good. How does it help you that he goes to so many meetings? *(Relational exception question, accepting where the family began the interview)*

Mother: I learn from what he learns there. I stay home with him. *(Pointing to her son)*

I suddenly realized that I was the only one in the therapy room aware of their child's activity. He was noisy, attempted to interrupt both parents, ran around the room, and was generally into everything. Neither parent appeared to notice these behaviors or seemed to want to address them. Their focus was on sobriety, and I had to trust them to know the order of their own business. I decided to let the boy go on doing "kid things"; if he became too disruptive, I would see whether this family knew how to correct itself without my advice.

Therapist: You have come to therapy to do what?

Mother: We just have to stay sober. That's it; I hit what they call bottom on the unit here, and I can't do what I was doing before. Because this time it will kill me.

Father: Been drunk for twenty years. It's over for me too.

Therapist: So how long have the two of you managed to stay sober?

Mother (laughing): Just this week.

Father (looking serious): Just this whole week.

Therapist: Great! How did you do this?

Father: A meeting every day, call my sponsor, and read the Big Book.

Mother: I use the Serenity Prayer, because I have lots of things to do and I can't always stop to go to a meeting. I read the Big Book and my meditation book. Use the slogan "One day at a time" a lot, too. We keep it simple.

Therapist: How do these things help?

Father: It's all new to me—I never saw things this way. Helps me get through the hard times.

Mother (nodding vehemently): See, I know what he's going through because I'm going through the same thing too. We are really scared of the same things.

Father (nodding): That's right.

Therapist: How does knowing what he's going through help the two of you stay sober? *(Relational exception question)*

Father: We talk about it, and she helps me when I can't see where I'm going to fall, and I help her the same way. I remind her: "One day at a time," and that helps her.

Mother: And I remind him of the meeting times. We're still scared to death, you know.

Therapist: Of course. What do you think you are doing that helps you to get through the scary times?

Mother: I have to stop myself and remind myself he's not fussing; that he's doing the best he can right now. When I do that, I can listen.

Father: I stop what I am doing and I look at her. Then I can get it. Looking at her reminds me of where we've been.

This conversation was about their strength and how they had come together to help one another stay sober. It was also about the power that a simple look at his wife had for this man.

In the meantime, their son was growing louder as he continued to roam around the room. His parents remained oblivious to him. He entered the bathroom next to my office and urinated on the wall, leaving the door open while he relieved himself. Still no one noticed him. He then paraded around the room, singing one repeated phrase to himself: "Where is the merry-go-round?" He sang this monotonous phrase over and over. Despite this uproar, I continued to search for all the things that had empowered his mother and father to maintain sobriety for the last week.

In the intervention, I used their views of the problem and praised them for acknowledging their fears. I noted that this was a realistic response to the beginning of a sober life and that it was wise of them to see it. I also complimented them on their willingness to get help from each other and to pay attention to those times when the other was having trouble. Their homework was to do all the things that were already working, notice anything else that worked, and come back the next week and report on these to me. They readily agreed to this.

Since they had ignored their son, I did not address his behavior; rather, I chose to recognize his interest in merry-go-rounds. I complimented the child on coming in with his parents and offering the report on who was sober. I gave him the homework task of repeatedly asking his parents the question: "Where is the nearest merry-go-round?" He smiled and complied by asking his father this very question as they left the room.

What was the rationale for this intervention? First, I let go of any assumptions I had about what this family needed to do to heal. They were the experts on their own lives; their own wisdom would outline each step. I saw my job as one of reinforcing the steps they were taking as legitimate ones in the recovery process.

Second, I noticed that the child seemed to be in charge of the family. I knew that this was a common situation for addicted families; readjusting this imbalance was another area where his parents would need to "recover." Rather than try to make this adjustment for them, I thought that they would be better off approaching parenting on their own terms, making errors and achieving success in their own way and time.

Their son's contribution turned out to be an essential one. By giving him the "homework" of asking his parents about the nearest merry-go-round, I was using what he brought to the session in a way that gave him a chance to return to childhood and be involved with the normal things that children are involved with. In any case, he was clearly a part of what went on in the session; I wanted to honor what he had brought, and his search for the missing merry-go-round was the obvious choice. I hoped that it would be enough to unlock his part in the family wisdom.

The second session brought some new work to do.

The family had succeeded in another week of sobriety, and we discussed what they had done to make that possible. They reported that their previous strategies had continued to work and that the mother had attended some meetings herself. Dad reported the whereabouts of the nearest merry-go-round and stated that he and his son had played on it.

They had a new goal, however. On their own this week, still sober and feeling cautiously hopeful about their progress, the couple had discovered that their communication wasn't so good. Communication was the issue they wanted to work on in the second session.

This development surprised me; I had thought that we would be staying with sobriety for a while. How did the issue of communication fit in?

They put it this way: maintaining sobriety was still their number one goal; although they had strategies that were working to help keep them sober, their way of communicating was getting in the way of these strategies. This made communication seem to them the natural next issue to address.

Since they had stayed sober, I decided to trust their judgment and explore the new issue they had raised.

Therapist: So, what has to be different with your communication?

Father: I yell at her before I can think about it. She yells back or ignores me. That doesn't help.

Mother: He doesn't see all that I have to do. I yell at him, too. And cuss him sometimes.

Father: It's bad, too. Could go on for hours. Has in the past.

There are a number of ways to approach this sequence to search for strength. I could have begun by asking any of these groups of questions:

- Are there times when you don't yell back at him? What do you do instead?

- Were there times when the yelling wasn't as bad as this week? What were you doing differently at those times?

- If you were to compare this week with last week in the area of communication, what would be better this week? How do you account for the difference?

- On a scale of one to ten, with one being poor and ten being very good, where would you put yourselves last week in terms of your ability to communicate? How about this week, where would you put yourself on this same scale? What did you do that made the difference?

- Were there times this week when you started to yell and caught yourself and overcame the urge to do it? If so, what did you do instead of the usual yelling?

Rather than start with the assumption that all their approaches to communication were failures, I decided to begin by looking for the times when they had shown each other a glimmer of their wisdom, even though they might not have been able to recognize that wisdom when it appeared. I chose to ask the final set of questions from the list.

Mother: Only once, did I catch myself.

Therapist: What helped at that one time?

Mother: I just really looked at him . . . and I guess I saw him struggling to stay sober. Because usually I yell, and he drinks then. I saw him struggle with it this time. I felt sad and glad at the same time. It was real strange. Made me think: I want to make it, and I want him to make it.

Therapist: Dad, how about for you, were there any times that you caught yourself and did something different instead?

Father: Just one time. I yelled at her without thinking, like I used to, and she looked so surprised. I think I saw that it hurt her, and I know she's having what I'm having: a hard time. I just stopped.

Therapist: What did each of you do after you stopped?

Mother: I said the Serenity Prayer.

Father (simultaneously): I left the room and read my Big Book.

I was privately elated that at least on these two occasions they had been able to do something differently. The difference for both of them had already proved to be a power in their lives: the same techniques that had helped them maintain sobriety for two weeks were now being applied to other issues related to the health of their marriage.

Few other exceptions were found in the course of this interview; accordingly, their homework task was to pay attention to what helped them get through tough moments in their communication in the following week and come back and report on it.

What was happening with their son was also interesting. Although he confirmed his father's report that they had found the merry-go-round and played on it, he gave me no report on who was sober this week. He still seemed enticed by the same behaviors that he showed in the first session: he was loud, and he moved around the therapy room as restlessly as he had in our first meeting, yet he still listened to each word from both parents. His mother and father again seemed oblivious to him. I decided to include him in his parents' homework by asking him to watch for times when things were going better at home and come back and tell me about it. All three agreed to do the tasks assigned.

The third session brought a report of a display of violence that was used as an example of a "worst-case scenario" in chapter 10: after the father had hit the mother, the couple separated from each other, with each going to a different end of the house. Although this incident felt like disaster to me, they viewed it as a marked improvement over all the other battles they had known in the past. Accommodating their reaction and recognizing the strengths that it demonstrated required a shift in my thinking gears.

This same interview also produced additional material related to the couple's need to communicate better.

After three weeks of sobriety, the father's past had resurfaced, ready to haunt him, just in case he needed a reminder: the time had come for his court appearance to face his last DUI charge. He reported that he had been cranky and "evil" over it and that he had asked his wife to go with him to court. At first she refused, saying that she had too much to do: "After all, he got the ticket." This statement led to some discussion.

Therapist (to mother): Yes, he got the ticket. What did that mean to you?

Mother: At first, nothing. Then it dawned on me—it came to me that maybe he needed me to face the court thing. I knew I wouldn't want to face it alone. I'd want him there.

Father: I didn't want to go alone. I knew I'd done wrong. I just wanted her to come with me.

Therapist (to father): How would that help?

Father: Well, she knows what it's like to be a drunk and then when you're sober try to face all the bad stuff you've done. We help each other because we know what the other is facing. I talked her into coming with me.

Therapist: How did you do that?

Father: First, I let her tell me how she felt about it all. I listened.

Therapist (to both): Is this different for you?

Mother: Yes, and I gave him a chance to speak his mind, too—and I listened.

Therapist (to mother): How did you do that?

Mother: I told myself to wait to see what he has to say and how he feels about it. I also told myself it really wasn't my problem, but I could go and support him through it. I think that's what a good wife does.

This segment of the interview closed here, but not before they launched into another problem. In addition to the court hearing, which they had both attended, they had suffered a burglary in their home this week. They told me how they had let each other know how they felt about being violated.

Mother: Scared to death! I knew there was nothing I could do to change what happened.

Therapist: How did knowing that help you?

Mother: I stopped wanting to blame anyone—it just happened.

Therapist: What did you do to get through something you couldn't change?

Mother: I cried first, said my Serenity Prayer, and asked my husband for help.

Therapist: Did any of these help at all?

Mother: Yes, especially the last one. We talked about how to make our house safe and who would be responsible for what.

Therapist: Did your husband listen to you?

Mother: Yes, of course.

Therapist: How did you get him to do that?

Mother: I didn't blame him . . . I just cried, over and over: "What are we going to do?" I told him I was real scared too.

Therapist (to father): How were you able to listen to her when she was so upset?

Father: Guess I told myself that being upset made sense and the only important thing to do was make everything safe again. So she cried, and I let her do that. Then we started to fix the windows together and look for what was missing.

Therapist (to father): Did working together help you? Either one of you?

Both nodded their agreement. They hated what had happened, but were able to find strength in each other by holding back their own reactions and listening to one another. Both viewed this as improvement in their communication. Their homework task was to continue to pay attention to the rough times in their communication and watch what each other did to make communication easier. The son's task was to do the same.

I was intrigued by the fact that neither of them was yet interested in their six-year-old's behavior. As loud and disruptive as ever, he continued to escape their notice. I wondered when they would see him.

I told myself that they were moving in a direction that made sense to them and was beginning to make sense to me: the first priority was sobriety, and the second was getting along with each other. They were doing the things that the experts say are good to do: using the tools of the Twelve-Step program, feeling their feelings and sharing them, and attending meetings. They were taking responsibility for themselves and overcoming the urge to blame. All this looked like growth to me.

In the fourth session, parenting finally became an issue. With their sobriety going well and marital communication improving, they suddenly noticed that something was wrong with their son.

Mother: We want you to do something with him *(pointing to her son)*. He's out of control. *(Father nods his agreement)*

Therapist: How do you know?

Mother (in a huffy tone of voice): I don't think kids should act like this in public, do you?

Therapist (to both): How do you want him to act?

Mother: I want him to sit in his chair and be quiet.

Therapist: Who of the two of you does this better?

Mother: Makes him mind, you mean? He does. *(Pointing to her husband)*

Father: That's right.

Therapist (to mother): What does Dad do that makes him able to get Tim to mind?

Mother (rising out her chair and demonstrating the father's technique): He lifts him up and puts him in his chair, like this, and dares him to get up.

Therapist: And this works?

Mother: Yes. *(Showing no awareness that she has just used the father's method and that her son is now sitting quietly)*

Therapist: Do you like what he is doing now?

Both nodded their agreement with what their son was doing. As they did, he began to whimper.

Mother: I hate it when he cries. I feel so bad—guilty—like I really hurt him.

My unstated conclusion was that here was a sober mom, facing real issues of motherhood, maybe for the first time. In my presence, she had successfully stopped his rude and loud behavior and got him to sit still. She had instructed him to stay put in her best "mom" voice. And he did. The sole issue left to deal with seemed to be the guilt she felt for doing what she had to do. I asked her what she thought she ought to do with the guilt.

Mother: I have to stop listening to it, for one thing.

Therapist: How did you do that just now?

Mother: I reminded myself that he could behave like a heathen everywhere we went and it just wouldn't be good for him and would drive us crazy. Right?

Therapist: Right. How did that help?

Mother: I have to tell myself to help him. I am his mom. It's my job to show him what to do.

Therapist: This helps?

Mother: Yes, a little guilt is a small thing compared to him acting right. I have to tell myself he can hurt a little so he can act right when he's with other people. We don't raise heathens. (*Looking at father*)

Father: That's right, he's gonna do right.

Here again was a mother, newly in recovery, awakening to her own wisdom about the role of motherhood. She came up with solid advice for herself, and it worked in front of our eyes. I could not have told her how to do a better job.

It took two more sessions to get Tim to behave himself. In each of these, I asked both parents to use discipline that had worked before whenever it was necessary—and also to catch Tim doing something right as often as possible and give him a hug each time they caught him behaving well.

By the the sixth session, the three of them had begun to look like a family. Tim stopped calling his parents by their first names and began referring to them as Mom and Dad. His parents remarked that neither had told him to do this; he just started doing it. And they all liked it. As the mother announced, things were really going well on all fronts: sobriety, marital communication, discipline, and hugs. Her comment on these developments stunned me:

Mother: We think we are approaching normal, whatever that is. (*Father agrees with a slight nod*)

Therapist: How do you know?

Mother: We think we are doing what other families do.

I looked at father and son and saw this scene: the son was sitting on his father's lap, and the two of them were tracing a capital W on a notepad; the father was teaching his son to write. I noted that they were completely oblivious to me and any questions I had. They were about their own business.

This case ended after seven sessions; the family announced to me that they had graduated from therapy and wanted to celebrate with a vacation. They thought, they told me, that vacations were something "normal families do."

Case Note

"I can't make it stop." *Amber, a beautiful, somber nine-year-old, arrived at my office with her five-year-old cousin in tow. Amber's aunt was with them; she stated that Amber was living with her family because Amber's mother was a heavy drinker who was currently using alcohol and drugs and involved in a violent relationship with an alcoholic man. Amber's aunt wanted me to "educate" her niece about "alcoholism in the family." Amber had witnessed the drinking, the arguments, and the violence, and her aunt felt that Amber needed to learn about alcoholism "from a professional."*

My immediate thought was that this child would lead me to what she needed to know. All I had to do was follow.

Therapist: So, I hear your aunt wants you to know about alcoholism. Is that true?

Amber (nodding her head): She wants me to ask questions.

Therapist: She does? Is this a good idea?

Amber (again nodding her head): Yes.

Therapist: Well, how should we do this? Who do you want in the room?

Cousin (interrupting loudly): Me! Me! Me!

Amber (smiling in his direction): Just him and me.

Therapist: Good idea.

She seated herself on the couch beside me. She looked mildly distracted. Her cousin seated himself in a swivel chair and began to spin in circles.

Therapist: Well, what do you need to know?

Amber: Why do people drink?

Therapist: Many people—doctors, nurses, and others—think that it is a disease. Once some people start to drink, they feel like their bodies really need beer or wine or liquor. Do you know what it's like to be really hungry?

Amber: Yes. *(Wrinkling her face in disbelief)*

Therapist: Well, the people who really need it can't stop doing whatever it takes to get it. Their body gets used to having it, and they think they can't do without it. Their whole body needs it, like we need food when we are really hungry.

Amber: Are they sick?

Therapist: Yes, we think of them that way.

Amber: Do they have to have it?

Therapist: They think they do. And their bodies tell them that they need it, and all sorts of terrible things happen when they drink too much or can't get any at all. It really hurts everything they do. Their work and health, and how they eat and take care of themselves, and their children and family.

Amber: I know that. Why does my Mom yell at me and say she will hit me when she's drinking?

Therapist: It is the sickness that is yelling at you through your Mom. It's the sickness of alcoholism speaking through your Mom when she says she will hit you. She probably doesn't remember this, does she?

Amber: No, she doesn't remember. Can she stop drinking?

Therapist: Well, yes, but she has to really want to do that. No one can make her do it. When she says she will hit you, what do you do to help yourself?

Amber: Hide from her, call my aunt, go to my aunt's house.

Therapist: This helps you?

Amber: Yes, I tried this stuff, and I got away. The court still says I've got to see her.

I stopped the conversation and looked at the pained grimace on her face. I asked her, "How am I doing?" She raised her hand and fluttered it in the air to signal that I was just doing a "so-so" job. Her cousin began to sing as he continued to spin in the swivel chair.

Therapist: Feels awful, doesn't it?

Amber (nodding): Yes. Why does my mom go back to her boyfriend after he hits her?

Therapist: It's the sickness that helps her to think she needs to go back. Has he hit you or threatened to hit you?

Amber: No, just my mom. But he scares me.

Therapist: What have you done to make yourself safe?

Amber: Call my aunt to come get me and ask my mom not to drink.

Therapist: What worked?

Amber: Calling my aunt.

Her cousin was still spinning in the chair; when he tried to interrupt her, she simply quieted him in an adult manner and moved on to her next question. I was just at the point of becoming concerned about his disruptive effect on the session when it occurred to me that his spinning might somehow be useful, if I let it be. I gave up my need to change his behavior.

Amber: What's it like to be drunk?

Therapist: Well, you see that chair and Tommy. What would happen if he was spinning all day long and then tried to stand up?

Amber: He would be dizzy, and he couldn't stand up.

Therapist: That's very much like it.

Amber (incredulous): And people like this?

Therapist: Most people start out liking it, and then they get sick with it. They think they need it just to get through the day. Their bodies tell them they need it, too.

Amber: Why did God make beer?

Therapist: Now, that one I don't know. I think humans make it and then get too used to it and need it. I think they forget about God.

I stopped the conversation again and asked her how I was doing with her questions. She raised her hand again to signal that I had improved some. "Better," she said. Her cousin stopped spinning and began to listen.

Therapist: Feels awful, doesn't it?

Amber: Yes. *(Squinting)*

Therapist: What else do you need to know?

Amber: How come I think about it all the time?

Therapist: It's hard to think about anything else sometimes. Have you noticed that?

Amber: Yes. I think about it all the time. I want the drinking to stop. I can't make it stop.

Therapist: Yes, you are right, you can't make it stop. Only your mom can stop when she wants to stop. When you are not thinking about it, what are you doing instead?

Amber: Swimming, playing with him *(pointing to her cousin)*, playing the stereo.

Therapist: How do these things help?

Amber: I don't know, I just don't think about it when I am swimming and doing things I like.

Therapist: Are there other times when you do things that help you get through all this thinking about it?

Amber: When I help my aunt, or she reads to me or tells me she loves me.

Therapist: How do these things help?

Amber: I don't have to think about it then. I can rest from it. How come you know so much about this?

Therapist: I grew up in a family very much like yours.

Amber: Who did you talk to?

Therapist: Nobody.

Amber (squinching up her face): Ooh! Not even 911?

Therapist: We didn't have 911 in those days.

Amber: Ooh! What about the neighbors? Could you go to the neighbors?

Therapist: No, I couldn't do that. Nope, no neighbors.

Amber: Ooh! What did you do?

Therapist: Didn't talk about it.

I stopped her again and asked how I was doing with her questions. She replied: "You're doing good." The session was near an end, and I asked if she had any other pressing questions for that day. She replied that she couldn't think of any more questions. I gave her this inter-vention:

> *Therapist:* Amber, I am amazed at how many good questions you asked me about alcoholism today. It shows that you have thought a lot about it. I think it is good that you know how you feel and can ask for help. These are really smart things. Maybe the best thing you are doing for yourself is that you have learned to do other things that help you get through the hard times. Also you know that you can't stop your mom's drinking. That is very smart. Some people figure these things out when they are thirty-nine and you figured out a whole lot of things at nine. So, keep doing all the things that help you, like swimming, playing with your cousin, listening to your aunt, and anything else that has already helped. Most of all, remember that you can't stop your mom from drinking; that is something she will have to do herself.

As we left the session, I suggested she come back in two weeks. She responded immediately: "No, one week! I'll bring more questions. Okay?" Surely no one led the way but her. She articulated her needs masterfully. Fortunately for her, I had followed well.

Childhood Abuse

I have found that child abuse comes in as many different forms as there are individuals who engage in this behavior. A solution-focused approach can be usefully taken to abuse cases regardless of the client's age or type of problem. It is essential here for the therapist to set aside any preconceived notions and let the client explain how the world is for him or her; this is especially true if the therapist is also a survivor of childhood abuse. For the client who has survived abuse, telling his or her story will often be a healing event in itself, and the therapist must make certain that his or her own issues do not stand in the way.

Survivors of abuse, like those injured by alcohol and drugs, often find basic life events difficult to handle. Daily life becomes a series of unexepected discoveries, and these are often viewed as threatening obstacles or overwhelming chores. It is crucial here for the therapist to help the client set a specific goal and that the goal be achievable and measurable—that is, expressed in terms of something that the client can do, think, or feel.

Although the strengths and wisdom of clients who have lived through these kinds of situations are often extraordinary, most are unaware that they have any wisdom of their own. Further, they shy away from using their instincts, since the abuse itself has taught them a very different lesson: "Don't trust your eyes or ears and certainly not your gut." With a new client, I tell myself from the beginning to set aside my emotions and judgments and focus on understanding the client's view. It helps to remind myself that the client brings all that he or she needs for our day's work. And that's what we are doing: a day's work, not a life's work. Together, we work on today in relation to a specific therapeutic goal.

Case Note

"My sister is still there." *A six-year-old girl reported to one of our counselors that she had been raped by her mother's boyfriend. She remembered what she had done, at age four, to survive the trauma of this experience.*

Claudia: He did "it" to me and my sister.

Therapist: Did what?

Claudia: It. You know. Put his privates inside my privates. Her too. I saw it.

Therapist: How old were you?

Claudia: Four. I told my mom, but she didn't believe me. Said I was a liar.

Therapist: Were you ever able to get away from him?

Claudia: Yes. If I hid in my secret cave. I have a cave next to my house. And sometimes I went to my granny's house.

Therapist: How did you know when to do that?

Claudia: When he starts drinking and yelling, then I know I got to go. And I go. Got away bunch of times.

Therapist: What else did you do to help yourself?

Claudia: Talked to my puppy and Gracie.

Therapist: Who is Gracie?

Claudia: My friend.

Therapist: How did that help?

Claudia: I told myself that Gracie loved me and my puppy loved me too.

Therapist: And this helped?

Claudia: Yep.

Therapist: Anything else?

Claudia: I told the space police. They help kids.

Therapist: How did that help?

Claudia: Well, they listen to me when I talk.

Therapist: What else helped?

Claudia: I just told *you*. You do something.

Therapist: What do you think is a good thing to do?

Claudia: Tell the cops, okay? My sister is still there.

I was amazed at this child's coping ability. In the midst of very real horrors, she had found several things she could do to help her spirit stay alive and to keep herself out of harm's way at least some of the time. And now she had mustered her strength to reach out to the very person who could do something to change her situation. The appropriate reports were filed that same day; Claudia elected to continue seeing this counselor.

I find children's strength amazing and do not mind telling them so; they like to hear about their own strength. It helps them believe in themselves and grow further into their abilities.

In the following case, I worked with a male therapist; he and I traded places from week to week, with one of us behind the mirror with an observing team while the other was doing the therapy. The couple we were counseling chose which of the two of us would work with them each week.

Case Note

"I don't want to do it alone." *An adult female came to the clinic with her husband for couples' therapy. The presenting problem was a "lack of trust" that both were experiencing in their relationship. Although the wife's brother had abused her sexually in her childhood, she had never confronted him; like so many other survivors, she had kept the abuse a secret and tried to act as if nothing was wrong. Yet she was experiencing difficulties in a number of areas in her life, and both she and her husband had begun to feel that their marital problems were related to this past abuse.*

Therapist: What would it look like if Mae had more trust in you, Tom? What would she be doing differently?

Tom: She'd listen better; she would read her Bible more—see, we've just accepted the Lord. She would go to church more often.

Therapist (to Mae): What would Tom be doing differently if you had more trust in him?

Mae: He would listen better, too. Sometimes he does.

Therapist: Oh, really? When was the last time you noticed he was listening better?

Mae: Last night. I knew it because he put his book down and turned around and looked right at me when I was talking.

Therapist: How did this help?

Mae: When I noticed it, I lowered my voice. It made me think: "He's going to help me." See, I wanted to talk to him about confronting my brother, but I don't want to do it alone—

Tom (interrupting): I thought I could do it for her—go up to him and confront him—but it's up to her. I think she can do it. I'll be there as a safety net, for her to fall back on if he tries anything funny.

Therapist (to Mae): Does it seem to you that this will work when you are ready to confront him?

Mae: Yep. I've just got to know he's going to be there for me.

Tom: I'll be there.

Therapist (to Mae): What is it that you would have to see from Tom that would let you know beyond the shadow of a doubt that you can trust him to be there?

Mae: He's got to listen to me more, just like he did the other night. He can do it if he wants to.

Therapist (to Tom): Is she right? You can do this if you want to?

Tom: Yeah. I've got to want to.

Therapist: What do you need to see from Mae that will let you know that you really want to listen to her?

Tom: I want to hear a soft voice.

Therapist (to Mae): Can you do this?

Mae: When I want to.

Therapist: What would it take for you to want to?

Mae: I have to think that it helps him to listen. I've got to stop my mouth before it starts.

Tom: We both have to do that.

Therapist: What does it take for both of you to stop before you start?

Tom: I've got to think first about what's going to happen if I don't listen—we'll have trouble.

Mae: I guess he might be right—he listens better to me when my voice is soft. I have to think about how I sound.

The relational questions that the therapist asks search for exceptions in this couple's relationship. Having them answer questions about each other in this way draws out the strength they know together as a couple and explores how that strength comes out between them.

The couple came in for some twelve sessions. Trust remained the core issue, and it continued to grow between them. In the context of therapy and her relationship with her husband, Mae found a new strength, one that clearly said no to being used by others. We watched her apply this new strength, first at home with her family, then on her job, and then with the therapy team when she found she had issues with us around transferring to another therapist. By the end of the sessions, she was ready to confront her brother and to reengage in therapy with the male therapist when our clinic reopened for the summer.

It was apparent to me from this case that what was important to these clients was the nature of the therapy—how it was conducted and how they were treated—rather than which therapist handled any given session or who their therapists were as persons. Once again, the key was to accept the clients' lead: we asked them to explain their strengths to us, and this was a task they were glad to do.

12

The Twenty-Minute Interview

We increase what we celebrate.

Sylvia Stitt Edwards

We can celebrate health or pathology; that is our choice.

The twenty-minute interview format originated in response to requests from students who were primarily training to become school counselors. These students had studied counseling theories and methods and were eager to start their careers, only to find themselves with caseloads as high as 700 students. Most felt overwhelmed; they were lost without the tools they needed to do the job they yearned to do.

In exploring the possibilities for doing "counseling" in situations where the caseload numbers were astronomical, the most useful approach seemed to be to take a model that was already working, identify its essential elements, and design a shortened format to make use of these same elements. After numerous discussions with Insoo Berg, two different styles of twenty-minute interview emerged; the style presented here is one that I developed and used with therapy students who tested it in clinics and schools in Indiana.

The twenty-minute format can be used in many settings: it has been found to be useful in schools, hospitals and medical clinics, recovery programs, and outpatient and inpatient settings. It can be used in any clinical setting where there are many clients and the counselor is pressed for time. Note, though, that the large caseloads many counselors have is not the only purpose for developing a shortened interview format. The shorter interview also offers a service for those who can afford only a half-hour session, for those with transportation problems, and for those clients we call "difficult"who choose to show up for only part of the session.

My own view is that it is best to suspend judgment of these "difficult" clients. Within the therapy session, I take the view that clients are doing what they need to do and making the best choices that they can in any given moment; I feel that a consistent application of this principle justifies some flexibility in the usual structure of the therapy hour.

In theory, this attitude also applies to "no-shows." In general, when using this model and displaying this attitude, I have found missed sessions to be a rare problem. When therapy is regarded as an environment where clients' views are affirmed and clients' progress is celebrated, most clients show up every week—including those who did not want to come in for therapy in the first place.

The twenty-minute interview format has also proved particularly useful in interviewing referral sources—those individuals who have referred the client to therapy. Accordingly, specific guidelines and questions for using an abbreviated interview format with referral sources have also been included here. This interview helps assure that the referral source expects change for the client and agrees on the goal for therapy.

Either clients or the individuals who referred them may be interviewed face to face or over the phone. (Yes, over the phone: the twenty-minute format has been used successfully in telephone interviews with clients and with referral sources.) The format can be used with or without a team; since most therapists work without a team, the format presented here is for a therapist working alone.

With or without a team, the overall process and the information collected parallel the format in a fifty-minute session described in chapter 8. After an interview period of about fifteen minutes, the therapist takes a three-minute break to consider the case or to consult with the team observing the session. The final two minutes of the session are used to deliver the written intervention that the therapist derives from the client view, compliments, and types of exceptions noted. A goal for the therapy is determined in the first session, and all further sessions focus on this goal until it is attained.

Basic Guidelines for Using the Twenty-Minute Interview

Guidelines for working with clients (whether referred by others or self-referred):

1. Accept the client's view as his or her reality.

2. Flow with that view. Don't be tempted to try persuading the client to change it.

3. Discuss the problem to be solved in the client's language.

4. Search for exceptions to the problem condition. Make a list of the exceptions you find.

5. Use compliments and the client view to set the stage for the homework task.

7. Choose a homework task that fits the exceptions that were found.

Guidelines for working with the referral source:

1. Accept the referring individual's view of the situation as true for him or her.

2. Flow with that view. Don't try to persuade him or her to think otherwise.

3. Find something positive in the work that he or she has already done on the situation. Compliment his or her efforts. Use the language that the referring person uses.

4. Search for times when the referring person thought that the situation was better. Ask how he or she helped to make the situation better.

5. Use compliments and the referring individual's view to set the stage for asking for his or her continued help.

6. Scale the referring person's willingness to continue to help.

Interviewing Clients: The Five Basic Questions

As the therapist listens to the client's story, he or she remains focused on the following five basic questions; these provide the path that the interview follows. I often open the original interview with the first question or weave it into the conversation in the first few minutes; in later interviews, I use the second and third questions early in the interview.

The questions take this form for self-referred clients:

1. What has to be different as a result of you talking with me? *(To set a goal)*

2. When was the last time you did this even a little better than now? *(To search for exceptions; ask this question several times)*

3. What were you doing differently at that time? *(To continue to search for strength; ask this question several times)*

4. On a scale of one to ten, with ten being very sure and one being not sure at all, how sure are you that you could do some of the things that helped you, if you really wanted to? *(To assess motivation)*

5. On that same scale, how likely is it that you will try some of these same things again soon?

For involuntary clients (clients who were referred to therapy) who appear "resistant" or "uncooperative," I determine the name of the referral source and then use this question first in the interview:

- What does *(the referring person)* say has to be different about you so that you won't have to come back and see me again?

Involuntary clients are often startled by this question: the therapist, an individual with whom they were prepared to struggle, has unexpectedly accepted their view of the situation. The combative response that they were ready to make is interrupted, and this interruption creates a moment of confusion in which the client must organize a new response. Cooperation often emerges from this confusion, as the new response rarely includes fighting with the therapist. The rest of the interview can make use of the questions outlined for voluntary clients.

Interviewing the Referral Source

Whether the referred client is in therapy voluntarily or involuntarily, I interview the referring source weekly to make sure that I am reaching the therapy goals that he or she wants to achieve. In effect, the referring person becomes a second client (Berg 1992) and often the more "serious" of the two; in the case of unmotivated or uncooperative clients, the referral source is usually the client most invested in seeing change occur. This regular interview, whether conducted by telephone or in person, can also help by letting the therapist double-check what the client has been saying about his or her progress and in determining when therapy is no longer needed. It helps to be certain that everyone agrees that the goal for therapy has been reached and maintained.

To make certain that our relationship is a cooperative one, I am careful to acknowledge the referring person's hard work on the problem thus far and his or her dedication to the client's well-being. Again, five basic questions provide a focus for the interview with the referring source:

1. What is the smallest change you can accept from *(the client)* at this time? *(To set a goal)*

2. When was the last time you found *(the client)* doing just a little bit better or a little more of what you wanted *(him or her)* to do? *(To search for exceptions)*

3. What was *(he or she)* doing differently at that time? *(List as many exceptions as possible)*

4. What do you think you were doing that helped *(the client)* to do more of this at those times? *(To search for more strength or exceptions)*

5. On a scale of one to ten, how willing are you to try some of these helpful things that you tried before?

Usually, the referring individual is willing to help. Accepting the referring source's views and finding compliments that fit often lead to an ounce more cooperation from a reluctant source.

Homework Tasks for the Client and the Referral Source

As in the fifty-minute interview format, the intervention closes each twenty-minute session. The therapist helps to create this "teachable moment" by accepting the view of the problem that the client or the referral source has, using the language that each of them uses to discuss the problem, and complimenting both on their efforts to solve the problem thus far. Each is then given a homework task.

The guidelines for assigning homework tasks following a twenty-minute session parallel those described in chapter 7 for a longer session:

- If the client or the referral source has tried several things that have worked in part, he or she is sent out to continue doing these things and asked to come back and tell how these strategies worked. (If an involuntary client and the referring person are in frequent contact, I also ask them to watch for any progress in each other and report on it as well.)

- If nothing has worked even a little bit or there are few exceptions, I send each person out to study themselves to see what works better in the next few days or weeks.

- When there are no deliberate exceptions, asking clients to study what helps them at all will invariably create new exceptions or reveal ways of getting through the situation. If no helpful things are accomplished to handle the problem, then the client can be asked: "How did you get by this time?" and the referral source can be asked: "How do you think *(the client)* got by this time?" Either the client or the referral source can be also asked: "How come you haven't given up?" or any of the other "worst-case" questions from chapter 10 for clients who are "just getting by."

Zona's case, which has been discussed in earlier chapters, provides a useful example of the process of developing complementary tasks for a client and the referral source. Throughout the course of eight twenty-minute sessions, the therapist worked closely with her mother, who had referred Zona for therapy.

Case Note

Zona. *The client was thirteen and obsessed with a rock star to the point that she could focus on nothing else; her mother was concerned because her daughter refused to attend school or arrived late and did nothing at home except lie around and listen to loud music.*

Therapist: What do you hope will happen to you here?

Zona: I guess we could get Mom off my back.

Therapist: Your mother suggested you come here?

Zona: She thinks I'm hopeless. I'm obsessed with New Kids on the Block—ooh, that Donny! Can't do homework, don't want to go to school.

Therapist: What does your mom want you to do differently?

Zona: Not think about it—him—anymore. I can't do that.

Therapist: When was the last time you were a little less "obsessed?"

Zona: What do you mean? I always think about it. Can't stop. He's so cool!

Therapist: When was the last time you were a little less obsessed?

Zona: You mean when I don't think about it as much?

Therapist: Is that when you are less obsessed?

Zona: When I am watching TV, I'm not thinking about him, unless he's on TV.

Therapist: When was another time when you weren't thinking about it so much?

Zona: When I talk on the phone and look at my homework at the same time—I don't think about him. And when I think about my dad—he's been gone since I was two. Don't know where he is.

Therapist: What was different at the times you weren't so obsessed?

Zona: I was watching TV, looking at my homework, and talking on the phone all at the same time.

Therapist: This helped?

Zona: Yeah.

Therapist: Anything else?

Zona: Nope.

Therapist: On a scale of one to ten, with ten being very sure and one being not so sure, how sure are you that you could do some of these things again, if you really wanted to?

Zona: Maybe eight, because I do them all the time.

Therapist: When do you think you will start?

Zona: You mean you think I can get better? I can't help thinking about it—him—them. I want to go to their next concert but I can't—my mom says because I won't stay in school. Wonder what Donny would think about me?

Zona's homework task after the first interview was presented in chapter 7: after ackowl-edging Zona's views of her mother's and her teacher's reactions to her problem, the therapist asked her to try all the things that had helped her be a little less obsessed and anything else that she could think of to try and to report back the following week on how those things had worked.

Zona's session was followed by the first of a series of ten-minute telephone interviews with her mother that were spread over the course of Zona's therapy. Here is a portion of that original interview:

Therapist: It seems that you have worked very hard on this problem with Zona. What's the smallest change you will accept from her at this time?

Mother: Well . . . she has to go to school. She's run me crazy with this concert and this Donny boy.

Therapist: Sure. When was the last time she got to school?

Mother: She went last Thursday and Friday.

Therapist: What did she do differently those days?

Mother: I don't know—nothing I can think of.

Therapist: Can you think of anything you did that might have helped her on those two days?

Mother: I yelled at her the night before and in the morning—we had a big fight. I don't want to do that again.

Therapist: Right. What else did you do that might have helped on the days she went to school?

Mother: I fixed her lunch and made her cut off the shower after ten minutes. That shower can run for a day with her in it. I also threatened to drive her to school and that seemed to get her moving. I don't know.

Therapist: How willing are you to try some of these things that may have helped her on those two days?

Mother: I'm worn out with her. I've got to see some change in her soon . . . and her self-esteem is so bad too, you know . . . .

Zona's mother's intervention read this way:

Therapist: I can appreciate how this has run you crazy, with the concert and Donny and all, and especially since you are worried about her self-esteem *(views of referral source)*. I am impressed that you haven't given up on her, even though she's run you crazy *(compliment)*. I am wondering if you would try some of the things that worked a little and anything else that comes to mind. I would like to call you at this time next week to see what progress you've picked up on in Zona and to make sure that we are working on the things you want us to be working on.

For both Zona and her mother, their individual points of view were appreciated and any efforts they had made to solve the problem were honored; each "client" was sent out to study herself and each other, and a progress report was requested for the next session. Zona's mother responded positively to her task and assured us that she would continue to do her part.

This case progressed to the point where Zona returned to school daily, began doing homework, lost her "obsession," and improved her grades and self-esteem. In a later session, she reported that the "obsession" had become a "mild interest," and she finally concluded that Donny would agree with her mother and tell her to stay in school. Therapy was terminated because both mother and daughter agreed that the initial problem had been solved, along with some related issues, and both were pleased with the outcome.

This case is not the exception. Problems have been solved by many clients, young and old, using the twenty-minute interview. If you are money conscious, time conscious or energy conscious, it's worth a try!

13

Applications to Other Settings

The most disastrous times have produced the greatest minds.

François August-René de
Chateaubriand

In our darkest moments, there is still the chance to see brilliance.

The solution-focused style of therapy is an application of a way of thinking about problems; as such, this same way of thinking can be applied to a wide range of dilemmas in many settings that deliver human services, whether to individuals, families, or larger groups. The solution-focused approach has been used successfully with school problems, discipline problems, drug and alcohol issues, eating disorders, employment problems, grief, sexual abuse, marital violence, issues related to terminal illness, chronic pain, attention disorders, and speech impairments, in addition to a wide range of psychological disorders.

This chapter looks at the application of the solution-focused approach to medical, educational, and employment settings. A brief discussion for parents who wish to use solution-focused strategies in the home is also offered.

In settings where time is limited, the shorter twenty-minute interview format (discussed in chapter 12) offers a chance to make services available to more clients. The basic guidelines for the twenty-minute format apply to each setting:

1. Accept the client's view as his or her reality. Flow with that view.

2. Use the client's language. Specify the problem to be solved in that language.

3. Search for strength by asking exception questions or worst-case scenario questions.

4. Identify strengths or coping strategies that can be repeated.

5. Acknowledge the client view, compliment client strength, and ask clients to engage in behaviors that have proved helpful to them.

6. If needed, set another time to meet with the client in the next few days.

Medical Settings

As earlier chapters have shown, the solution-focused model asks therapists to view their clients as the experts; the therapist is only a visitor in the client's world. What can a medical practitioner learn from this approach?

The diagnostic and treatment models that physicians learn in medical school take a very different approach. What the patient says or feels or does may or may not be significant; the "answers" are all in the doctor's hands—in his or her training and knowledge of the relationships between the patient's presenting problem and symptoms, observation and analysis of test results, and the resulting diagnosis and treatment plan. In this context, physicians and patients alike often come to view their relationship as one in which the doctor is the expert, and the patient is the passive recipient of that expert's care.

Modern medical practice recognizes that patients have a much more active role to play. This is particularly true for those health problems where the patient's cooperation is essential, as it is in any prevention or treatment plan requiring changes in diet or exercise or other behavior. Physicians who follow a "holistic" model also recognize the benefits of awakening the self-healing potential that involved patients have. As a client-centered approach, the solution-focused model clearly has strengths to offer in these areas.

At the same time, under the "managed care" approach many doctors, nurses, and other health staff are left with the role of providing services to more and more patients in shorter and shorter periods of time. Here again, the goal-oriented approach of the solution-focused interview format can help to structure many of the interactions that occur in providing health services.

I am acquainted with a number of physicians in general practice who make use of solution-focused techniques in solving problems and counseling their patients. Discussions with these professionals suggested a number of specific applications to a variety of medical settings. The ideas given here cover use of the twenty-minute interview format for common health problems, regular checkups, chronic pain, and terminal illness. Some suggestions are also given for working with patient groups.

Health problems. When health problems are identified, the caregiver can ask questions like these to assess patients' current strategies and their view of their treatment:

- What is the patient's goal in regard to the problem that has been identified?

- Is the patient's goal a realistic one? Can the problem be cured by some means, or must the patient find some way to cope with it?

- If a cure is a realistic goal, what has the patient already done that helps to reach this goal? What has the patient thought about doing? What else can be tried?

- If the realistic goal is to cope with the problem, what approaches has the patient already identified that help him or her cope?

- What else has the patient thought about doing?

A chiropractor friend asks these kinds of questions at the beginning of treatment and continues to ask them as therapy progresses. Scaling questions are used ("If you had one dollar's worth of pain at your first appointment, how much do you have now?") in conjunction with diagrams of the human body to assess the work that needs to be done each week. The questions scale the amount of pain the patient is feeling, and the diagrams let the patient outline the areas where work needs to be done.

Regular checkups. When the health caregiver's focus is on wellness or prevention issues, rather than health problems, solution-focused questions can be very useful in assessing a patient's ability to reduce risky behaviors such as smoking, alcohol consumption, drug use, unsafe sexual practices, improper use of medications, and poor eating, sleeping, or exercise habits. When a change in behavior is a goal, questions can focus on what patients are able to do to make themselves a little bit healthier than before. Questions similar to those used for health problems can be incorporated into a written assessment form or asked when the health practitioner interviews the patient. An example follows:

> *Doctor:* So how is it that you were able to cut down from three packs of cigarettes a day to one and a half packs a day?
>
> *Tom:* I listened to my lungs for once.
>
> *Doctor:* Hmm, how did that help?
>
> *Tom:* Well, I believe I'll quit coughing so much if I cut down. Didn't like what I heard.
>
> *Doctor:* What did you do instead of smoking so much this week?
>
> *Tom:* Chewed gum, smoked only half of a cigarette some of the time.
>
> *Doctor:* Would you like to hear your lungs now?

The doctor here takes Tom's idea of "listening to his lungs" and builds on it by letting Tom hear the actual rattle in his lungs. In the same way, the reasons that a patient gives for doing something positive can often be used by the physician to highlight the patient's strengths and draw on them to assist in the healing process.

Many common problems that patients experience can be met with this same question: "So, what are you doing that helped even a little bit?" If the behavior that the patient reports can be repeated and falls within the realm of what is realistic for the patient, then the patient's activity may enhance treatment. The key is to remember that the patient's behavior and treatment are not separate; if the connection between them is discussed and encouraged, they can work together.

Chronic pain. Despite their inability to relieve their symptoms, patients who endure chronic pain have not "given up" or surrendered to their condition; rather, they can be viewed as "experts" in coping. The most useful questions for these patients can come from the discussion of worst-case scenarios in chapter 10. The point for the health practitioner is to help the patient focus on what works at all. Here is a sample of how questions like these can work:

> *Nurse:* I see that you are having increased lower back pain again—from the accident, I guess.
>
> *Gloria:* Yes, it's really awful—worse than last time.
>
> *Nurse:* What are you doing now that helps even a little bit?
>
> *Gloria:* Nothing helps. Nothing works.
>
> *Nurse:* I see. If nothing works or helps, how are you getting through the day?

Gloria: I drink a lot of herb tea and use a heating pad.

If the nurse in this example pursues this question, she is likely to find a host of things that Gloria is already doing to "get by" in her situation. These strategies can then be "prescribed" as part of her treatment. This is not to say that Gloria's back pain is unreal. It is real, and the caregiver will want to acknowledge that it is. At the same time, the patient can be asked what she is doing to help herself, and her answers will help to assure that patient and caregiver are moving in the same direction.

Terminal illness. While no therapy can claim to reverse terminal illness, counseling can help patients finish life as they would like to do. Too often, persons who are dying lose touch with others, including those they are closest to, at a time when they need these contacts the most. While many of these patients die alone, with their feelings and wishes locked inside them, terminally ill patients often can and do make rich meaning out of the last moments in their lives.

Short, nontaxing interviews that are solution-oriented can be used to assess the patient's current outlook on life and identify current goals and any issues left to be resolved. Here is a part of an interview I had with an 83-year-old alcoholic who had been diagnosed with a terminal illness. Two incidents had already demonstrated his determination to use drinking and driving to end his life, and the interview took place in the Intensive Care Unit after his third attempt.

Therapist: So, what do you make of your third trip to ICU?

Al: I think I messed up—I didn't go this time. I will just try again.

Therapist: So you really want to go next time, huh?

Al: Yes. I'm tired.

Therapist: How do you explain that you didn't make it this time?

Al: I told you. I messed up.

Therapist: What do you think keeps you going at all?

Al: Well, I am worried about Sara *(his daughter)*.

Therapist: What has to be done with Sara?

Al: I want her happy again. She's depressed.

Therapist: What do you want done about that?

Al: I want you to take care of it for me.

Therapist: Sara wants you with her, and all of this is really scaring her. What can you do to stop scaring her?

Al: She wants me to agree to go into a home, instead of living by myself. That is crazy.

Therapist: Sara is pretty stuck on the idea. What can you do to convince her otherwise, that she's wrong about you?

Al: Nothing, really. I guess I will have to go live with people I don't know.

The rest of the interview was spent preparing for a family interview and nursing home placement. We looked at times he had done things he hated doing and how he had been able to do those things. I agreed to work with his daughter on her depression. He expressed relief that she would get the help that he wanted her to have.

Group work with patient groups. I have found that using solution-focused ideas can be an uplifting experience in groups facing even the most difficult issues. A shared awareness of each other's strengths breeds more strength and powerful wisdom among group members.

Practical experience in numerous groups has helped me to develop a number of helpful assumptions about the process that groups typically follow. I use these guidelines to make sure that the group has a context within which it can unfold and as a compass to chart a course for my own interaction with the group.

- I remind myself that people will take what they need from the group. What they need does not have to come from me.

- I acknowledge each person in the group and any contribution, no matter how small.

- I accept each group member's viewpoint.

- I remind myself that groups have the power to self-correct.

- I remember that the message of strength is highly contagious and that I can be most helpful by asking questions about strength. Good questions will keep the group focused on its task.

I take suggestions for group topics from patients, doctors or therapists, and any other staff members. It is generally easier to get the cooperation of a patient group if the group members choose the topic. The following general questions can be explored by groups facing a wide variety of issues:

- The last time you faced _____, what did you do that helped you get through it?

- What else helped you get through it?

- If you had to face it again, what ideas did you get from group today that you think might help?

The group leader should make the rounds of the group, letting the conversation flow where the members take it. It helps to ask each person the first two questions, taking care to acknowledge any response from a patient, including what looks like no response. Be sure to leave time before the meeting ends to affirm everyone's part in the group and offer appropriate compliments to each. Homework tasks can be assigned if group members ask for them or come up with suggestions of their own. The homework tasks come, of course, from what has helped them or what they think might help them.

Educational Settings

Few individuals with experience in eduactional settings view teaching as a one-way transfer, with the content of any given class simply poured into the waiting receptacle of passive and more-or-less malleable students. To the extent that any material requires active student participation, solution-focused techniques can become a useful adjunct to other techniques for developing discussion and activity groups and for one-on-one learning situations.

Although school counselors are expected to specialize in the kinds of problems that arise during school hours, a host of other personal issues can affect how students behave and perform in the classroom. Children and teenagers are accustomed to spending around thirty hours a week in school, and students with crises or long-term family problems at home often turn to teachers and school counselors for help. For school counselors with heavy and varied caseloads, a solution-focused approach may be the most viable alternative.

The discussion here focuses on use of the solution-focused model in school counseling situations, in carrying out disciplinary actions, in developing classroom guidance exercises and discussion groups, and in leading small skill-building and learning groups.

School counseling situations. The twenty-minute interview has proved very useful in individual counseling sessions for many types of problems. In addition to the personal problems that many clients bring to school counselors, such as child abuse, sexual abuse, grief and loss, depression, or low self-esteem, these include issues specific to school settings, such as attention or attendance problems or inappropriate classroom behavior. The twenty-minute interview can be used by teachers, counselors, aides, administrators, and school psychologists.

If less than twenty minutes are available to solve a problem, these three questions can be helpful to start a short discussion:

1. When you were dealing with this problem better, what were you doing differently?

2. How did you do that?

3. What was better for *you* when you did handle it better?

The first question is an exception question and can be used to get a list of strengths. Asking the second question forces the student to account for his or her own strength. The third question asks the student to think about the positive payoff for changing.

Note that these questions do not have to be asked in a formal counseling or office setting. They can be asked "on the run" and have been used in hallway conversations, at the lunch table, and in many other settings.

Counselors and teachers may find it helpful to make use of a referral form similar to the one included here. One side of the form is filled out by the teacher when the student is referred to the school counselor, and the other side is completed by the student, either at the time the referral is made or at the start of a twenty-minute interview with the counselor.

When the student's appearance in the counseling office is clearly not a voluntary one, the counselor can begin the interview by asking the student: "What will you have to do to get everybody off your back?" Some counselors may find it helpful to ask teachers to use differently colored forms for voluntary and involuntary student referrals. These color-coded forms let counselors and administrators know at a glance what kind of problem is headed their way.

Disciplinary action. Components of the twenty-minute interview can be used to develop an expedient method of discipline with the student as active participant. Administrators and teachers can use these questions in handling discipline problems with a student:

- What is *(the referring person)* saying you did wrong?

Referral for Counseling

Student's name _____ Date _____

What change do you want to see in this student after counseling? _____
_____
_____

What was the student doing when this problem was a little bit better? _____
_____

What were you doing that may have helped it be a bit better? _____
_____
_____

_____
Teacher's signature

The teacher completes the front of this form, and the student fills out the other side.

To be completed by student

What problem has to be different after counseling? _____
_____
_____

When the problem was better, what were you doing differently? _____
_____
_____

On a scale of one to ten, how likely is it that you can change if you want to?
_____
_____

_____
Student's signature

- What is the behavior that you think you have to change?

- What is it that your teachers *(or parents or principal)* want you to do differently?

- The last time you overcame the urge to behave this way, what were you doing differently? How did that help?

- If you wanted to, how sure are you that you could *(do what the student was doing differently)* again?

- What are you willing to do now?

Before the disciplinary action is determined, use this intervention:

I understand that you feel *(insert student views)*, and I am impressed that you faced this with me, as well as by *(add one or two more compliments)*, so I would like you to help me determine what action we need to take now to help you avoid a run-in with this person again. I would like for you to try all the things that have worked for you when you overcame the urge to behave in this way. And because the rules here say that some kind of consequence must happen when people behave this way, I would like to hear what you think is a reasonable discipline for you.

When students are given a choice in their discipline, I have noticed that they are harder on themselves than I would be and that they actually follow the punishment. They are more cooperative and are more likely to ask for help in the future before the fact rather than after the fact. When the disciplinary process treats the student with respect, the relationship that the student has with the counselor tends to stay intact and on good terms.

If the student's suggestion for punishment is an unrealistic one, the counselor or administrator can ask what problems the student foresees will arise in attempting to carry it out. When students are asked to study the feasibility of their choices, more often than not they make the needed adjustments or simply come up with another alternative for their discipline.

Most of us feel uncomfortable when we are asked to discipline or punish others; neither we nor the students are doing something we necessarily want to do. I have found it helpful to draw on this discomfort and let students know that we are "in the same boat"; we are all accountable, and we all have to follow the same rules. In this way, our shared task of identifying an appropriate punishment binds us together.

Students fare better when disciplinarians take time with them. Somehow the guidance that comes through in this kind of disciplinary interview translates as "Here is someone who cares" or "Here is someone who has time for me." For many students, these caring moments may be the only ones they get.

In one case, many years ago, a group of teenage boys were in the habit of getting in trouble every morning at their junior high. The principal was livid with exasperation when he called me into his office for a consultation. These boys, he told me, were spending 90 percent of their school days in his office, beginning very early every morning. What could be done?

A brief investigation turned up the fact that all of these boys were from fatherless homes; observation suggested that the boys actually liked the reactions they were getting from the principal. When he disciplined them, they would carry out the punishment he assigned and come back for more.

I thought of their interaction as a flow of energy: right now, it was going in a negative direction, but it could just as well and just as easily flow in a positive one.

I told the principal that I thought his strength was what they needed in their lives, seeing that none of them had clear examples at home to follow. I suggested an alternative to him: instead of waiting for disaster every morning, he could take the initiative and "get it over with," perhaps for the day. He agreed to try meeting them as they entered school each morning with a personal "checkup" for each of them.

He was surprised to find that the boys not only began to settle down, but were soon eagerly searching him out each morning. They lost the need to get in trouble and began to develop the habit of listening to the principal's guidance before trouble started. Their relationship with each other changed markedly for the better.

Classroom guidance and group activities. Questions from the twenty-minute interview format can be coupled with content material from many types of established curriculum. The format is especially useful for topics such as grief or loss, drug or alcohol use, eating disorders, suicide, arguments with parents, and low self-esteem, as well as classroom discussion of problems with behavior or grades. The teacher or counselor will find it helpful to follow these guidelines:

1. Choose a topic relevant to the students' lives (or let the students choose one).

2. Have the students form a circle where everyone can see everyone else.

3. Make sure each student has the needed supplies for the group experience.

4. Pay close attention to each student's contribution to the group. You may want to take notes, list contributions on a blackboard, or assign students the task of keeping a record of the discussion.

5. If appropriate, incorporate other modes of expression, such as drawing, listening to music, or role playing, into the group experience.

6. Close by praising each student for his or her contribution and reviewing the topic covered.

Solution-focused questions can be used to start the discussion or as a follow-up to role playing or other activities. It is very important to accept each student's response—including any feelings expressed and the student's behavior in the group. Keep in mind that some subjects are hard to deal with and that each student is doing the best that he or she can.

The following questions are appropriate for a classroom discussion of loss and grief. After each question, the group leader should wait for a number of students to respond and acknowledge each individual response.

- Who has lost something or someone they loved?

- How did you feel at the time?

- What helped you get though this time?

- What else helped you to get through this loss?

The counselor or teacher should end the group by praising each student for his or her contribution. Finding a wealth of material to compliment is rarely a difficult task, as students are usually eager to discuss issues relevant to their lives, and their responses to questions like these are often nothing short of amazing. Students who have been quiet throughout the discussion can still be praised for "listening well." Those who have reacted to the discussion by showing "resistant" or "oppositional" or "misbehaving" attitudes can be complimented for their willingness to show how they "really feel."

Behavior problems are rarely encountered once the group has begun. The questions have a trancelike power, and group members tend to stay focused on the business at hand. Even students who seldom participate in class discussions are eager to listen when classmates share personal experiences. The entire group seems to gain from each other's attempts at coping and to grow from individual members' strengths and successes.

A counselor who has been invited into a classroom will do well to end by thanking the teacher for the class's time and any level of participation the teacher has offered. When students are thanked for their participation, they often look forward to the next visit from the school counselor, regardless of the difficulty of the material to be covered. And so it is with teachers as well.

Once a relevant classroom activity appropriate for the age of the students has been selected, films, filmstrips, videos, prepared curriculum, popular songs, cartoons, and a host of other media may all be used to present a pertinent idea and spark discussion. The form for a Group Activity Plan provided here can be used to record the materials and the type of solution-focused questions used and to track student responses.

In evaluating student responses, the counselor should consider the types coping strategies that students have described. If most of the exceptions that students introduced were deliberate ones, these activities can be reassigned. If most of the exceptions are spontaneous ones, then students can be assigned the "homework" of paying attention to what they are doing when the problem is better, and follow-up group activity can be planned to evaluate the results.

Small-group learning and skill building. When students are having difficulty learning skills or new tasks, solution-focused questions can help them draw on past successes in tackling difficult learning tasks. As before, the process of cooperation in a learning environment begins with the leader's acceptance of each student's view of his or her own situation. When a student agrees with the praise that the leader gives to an area of strength, acceptance intensifies and brings about a higher level of cooperation. Here are some useful questions that students can answer, either individually or as a group:

- What was the hardest thing you ever learned to do?
- What helped you to learn how to do it?
- What was the first step you took?
- What did you have to do to get started?
- What were the other steps you had to take?
- What steps do you need to take now to learn the new skill?
- Who will be the first person to notice that you have learned it?
- What will be the first clue that will tell you that you are doing better with this new skill?

Discussion can be followed by a guided meditation that asks students to visualize themselves doing the difficult task. The following meditation may be combined with soft music for use in a variety of learning situations:

Close your eyes and breathe in deeply. Allow the muscles in your head
to relax. Pretend you are floating on a cloud. Let your shoulders,

Group Activity Plan

Content _____

_____

_____

Resources used _____

_____

_____

Ages and number of students _____

The teacher's view of the situation under consideration _____

_____

_____

Type of solution-focused questions used:

Type I	Type II
1. The last time you handled this a bit better, what were you doing differently?	1. Suppose you had magic and this problem was all better, what is the first thing you know you will be doing differently?
2. How did you come up with that?	2. When was the last time you did this a little better?
3. What did others notice about you at that time?	3. What was better for you at this time?

Student responses _____

_____

_____

stomach, legs, and arms relax. See yourself at a time when things were going well. See yourself doing something you thought was very difficult. Continue to breathe deeply. Remember how you felt then. See yourself making progress and remember what you did to move ahead. See the faces of those around you as you continue to move toward your goal. Remember what it is about you that lets you succeed. Continue to breathe deeply. See yourself reaching your goal and feel what it means for you to succeed. See yourself doing your very best. Remember now what it takes from you to do this well. Figure out what you must do first, second, and third in order to do your best. When you are ready, return to this room. Open your eyes and tell yourself what you now need to do to succeed.

Employment Settings

Changing jobs is one of the most stressful experiences that anyone in our society can undergo. While clients may be hampered by a lack of the skills and information that an employment counselor can offer, the counselor should keep in mind that the effects of stress also hinder a successful job search. Counseling is inevitably more effective when the counselor keeps the client's attitudes and feelings in focus at each stage of the process. When large caseloads limit the amount of time available, it is also simply more efficient to accept the client's views, rather than engage in a battle to change them.

Solution-focused ideas and questions can be applied successfully to a wide range of issues that clients face in employment settings, including counseling job applicants and conducting employment interviews, coping with underemployment or job loss, returning to employment after years of homemaking, and so on.

Counseling job applicants. Job applicants can benefit from a chance to tell something of their stories just as much as clients in other settings. In addition to the usual vocational testing, interest inventories, and requests that the applicant list strengths related to jobs under consideration, questions regarding the client's views can readily be incorporated into an employment interview of any kind.

For the repeat applicant, the interviewer can use these questions:

- The last time you landed a job, what helped you do it? *(Ask several times)*

- How did you manage to do this? *(Repeat after each exception)*

- What did it take to get you started?

- What will it take for you to get started now?

For the first-time applicant, these same questions can be modified in this way:

- What things have you heard that you have to do to get a job these days?

- Which of these things do you know how to do already?

- What did you have to do to learn these things?

- How confident are you in doing them now?

- What else do you think you need to learn to get your next job?

- What else can I help you with?

Whenever a client is asked to assess strengths that have helped accomplish goals in the past, the effect is the development of self-appreciation and a desire to cooperate, closely followed by hope. When these attributes are combined, clients want to move forward. All three lead to perseverance, just what is needed in the job market today.

Job loss. Although no one in today's economy seems immune from the risk of unemployment, the meaning attached to the loss of a job varies from client to client; the counselor or employment interviewer must set aside any preconceptions or personal fears that he or she may have. For most, the loss of a livelihood brings real hardship and worry, often together with a loss of self-confidence and a wide range of other reactions. It is critical that the counselor listen closely to the language the client uses and be alert for any hint of strength that emerges as the client speaks. Inevitably, the story will be a tough one; yet, in undergoing the events of their lives, the meaning that people choose to give them serves as a bridge to new ways of coping. By staying attuned to that meaning, the counselor will help assure that the client's ability to cope is highlighted and brought into focus.

The questions that follow help search for the meaning of job loss in the life of one client.

Therapist: You have really been through some tough times lately. I am amazed that you've held up under all the pressure.

Colt: You have to hold up. There's no work. But I can't give up.

Therapist: What does it mean to you that you have lost your work now?

Colt: I think I've lost one way to do things, and it feels like the only way I know. It feels scary, because I'm older. If I was younger, this would be easier.

Therapist: What keeps you going now?

Colt: Knowing that I can't give up. My family keeps me going too.

Therapist: How is that?

Colt: Knowing they are with me—that they have hope that things will change even when I don't have hope. They tell me not to give up.

Therapist: How does listening to them help you now?

Colt: Well, I know I am not alone, and I have a goal when I see them.

Therapist: When was the last time you had to look for work?

Colt: About ten years ago now.

Therapist: What did you have to do then to get a job?

Colt: Took a bunch of tests, got some training, and I guess we moved then too. Yep, we moved.

Therapist: What have you heard that you have to do nowadays to get work?

This interview continued in this way, searching for all the strength that Colt had used or had thought about using. The interview ended with a list of steps that he could take on his own behalf to alleviate his situation. His mood lifted and he appeared ready to tackle the search.

As with the use of solution-focused techniques in other settings, compliments that the client believes to be true are crucial parts of any "homework" or action steps that the counselor assigns. Compliments that are generally useful include such strengths as "not giving up" or "sticking with the process" and a willingness to "keep on trying" or "try lots of things." Any hint that the client's self-esteem is evident or thriving can be highlighted by the counselor.

Groups for unemployed persons. As with individual clients, it is essential for the group leader to allot enough time for individuals in the group to describe their current situations and the meaning that each has derived from his or her experience. The group leader must note each person's reactions and pay attention to the strengths that each displays. Whatever each individual offers in the group, the leader can appreciate it, affirm the difficulty faced by each client, and respect even minimal attempts to cope.

Questions like these can help trigger empowering discussions at a time when group members often feel powerless:

- What particular situation brought you to the group?

- What is a reasonable goal to expect from yourself at this time?

- What helps you to cope as you are out of work? *(Ask many times)*

- The last time you found yourself out of work, what did you do to get back to work?

- What new things have you thought about trying in addition to the things that helped before?

- What are you willing to do now to help yourself? *(Ask client to make a list)*

Another variation of these questions can also be helpful:

- What does it mean to each of you to lose your job now?

- When was the last time you felt this way?

- What did you do then to help yourself through that time?

- What else have you thought about doing that might help?

Questions like these can be assigned as an individual writing assignment, to be completed at home and discussed in group, or coupled with a simple guided meditation similar to the one provided in the section on small-group learning and skill building earlier in this chapter. Similar questions can also be combined with career and vocational testing and interest inventories.

Perhaps the most helpful technique is to ask clients to create a list of action steps based on successes in their lives. When group members share any bit of success they experience, they offer hope to the group as a whole and hope for others to generate their own solutions.

For Parents

What we say to our children has a powerful influence on their lives. "Difficult" children and "problem kids" tend to hear a great deal about their mistakes and their weaknesses—and even "good kids" tend to hear relatively little about their strengths and abilities. Taking a solution-focused approach to problem solving is a good way for parents to turn that flow of negative energy around.

Parents who focus on their children's strengths send them a powerful message—and a message that may otherwise not be heard, as parents are often the only significant source of praise in a child's life.

The first step is simply to make a commitment to catch your child doing something well as often as possible. The next step is to make sure that the child hears your appreciation and knows what it is that he or she is doing well. We can relieve a heavy focus on deficits in any child by highlighting what is working, even if the positive aspect is just a moment in the child's whole day.

At home, the benefits are enhanced cooperation, an open and communicative relationship, and an enhanced ability to listen on the part of parent and child. These benefits in turn make it easier to resolve problems and develop new skills and abilities.

Here are some questions for parents to use that help children to work at solving problems:

- Do you understand what I am asking you to do?

- What is the reason I want you to do this?

- What do *you* think you should do about this problem?

- The last time you found this hard to do and you did it anyway, what helped you do this?

- What else helped?

- What can I do that will help you to want to do what I ask?

Regardless of the problem, a resolution is invariably easier to reach if the child knows that the parents are seeing what he or she does well and honoring the efforts being made.

The solution-focused approach also reminds us to respect our children's developing sense of themselves. The independent opinions and beliefs that older children begin to form can seem threatening to parents; often, parents feel an urge to simply tell their children what to think and feel in order to prevent them from "making mistakes" or "embarrassing themselves." While a protective or controlling strategy may seem the safest in the short run, in the long run children will usually develop their own attitudes and act these out anyway.

If there is a cherished space in parents' lives for their children's own opinions and attitudes, then their children will try on many different beliefs to see which ones fit. They will discard those that do not work and keep what is a proper fit for them. They will grow into what fits them naturally.

Parents who forego the need to impose their own attitudes free the creative capacities of their children. This approach allows children to learn how to take care of their own needs and to trust their own ability to do so. Beyond that, when children are honored for who they are and respected for their efforts, they are more likely to cooperate with parents and accept help from them. On the inside, they can muster their own wisdom because it has been called for early in their lives. Their inner wisdom has been trusted by their most cherished loved ones. Under these conditions, their inner wisdom becomes a trusted inner friend and ally in all they do.

A Beginning . . .

The words here are the first steps in a long journey to understand how people change. They present one way to see change.

The words here are the first steps in a long journey to appreciate difference. They describe one way to respect difference.

The words here are first steps toward knowing the power of therapy and toward understanding how people empower themselves. They point toward one way to offer help, and one way that persons find their inner wisdom.

The words here are a beginning.

Bibliography

Berg, I. 1985. "Helping Referral Sources Help." *The Family Therapy Networker* 9 (3): 59-62.

———. 1988. "Couple Therapy with One Person or Two." In *Troubled Relationships*, ed. E. W. Nunnally, C. S. Chilman, and F. M. Cox, 30-54. Families in Trouble Series, vol 3. Newbury Park, CA: Sage.

———. 1989. "Of Visitors, Complainants, and Customers: Is There Really Any Such Thing as Resistance?" *The Family Therapy Networker* 13 (1): 21.

Berg, I., and S. Miller. 1992a. "Working with Asian American Clients: One Person at at Time." *Families in Society: The Journal of Contemporary Human Services* 73 (6): 356-363.

———. 1992b. *Working with the Problem Drinker: A Solution-Focused Approach.* New York: Norton.

de Shazer, S. 1975a. "Confusion Technique." *Family Therapy* 2 (1): 23-30.

———. 1975b. "Brief Therapy: Two's Company." *Family Process* 14 (1): 79-93.

———. 1977. "The Optimist-Pessimist Technique." *Family Therapy* 4 (2): 93-100.

———. 1979. "On Transforming Symptoms: An Approach to an Erickson Procedure." *American Journal of Clinical Hypnosis* 22 (1): 17-28.

———. 1982a. *Patterns of Brief Family Therapy: An Ecosystemic Approach.* New York: Guilford.

———. 1982b. "The Use of Teams in Family Therapy." In *Questions and Answers in the Practice of Family Therapy*, ed. A. S. Gurman, vol. 2, 296-298. New York: Brunner-Mazel.

———. 1982c. "Some Conceptual Distinctions Are More Useful Than Others." *Family Process* 21:71-84.

———. 1984a. "The Death of Resistance." *Family Process* 23 (1): 11-21.

———. 1984b. "Mark Twain Did Die in 1910." *Family Process* 23 (1): 20-21.

———. 1984c. "Brief Family Therapy: A Metaphorical Task." *Journal of Marital and Family Therapy* 6 (4): 471-476.

———. 1985. *Keys to Solution in Brief Therapy.* New York: Norton.

————. 1986. "A Requiem for Power." *Contemporary Family Therapy* 10 (2): 69-76.

————. 1987. "Minimal Elegance." *The Family Therapy Networker* 11 (8): 57-60.

————. 1988a. *Clues: Investigating Solutions in Brief Therapy.* New York: Norton.

————. 1988b. "Utilization: The Foundation of Solutions." In *Developing Ericksonian Therapy: State of the Art,* ed. J. Zeig and S. Lankton, 112-124. New York: Brunner-Mazel.

————. 1989. "Resistance Revisited." *Contemporary Family Therapy* 11 (4): 227-233.

————. 1990. "Erickson's Systemic Perspective." In *The Broader Implications of Ericksonian Therapy,* ed. S. Lankton, 6-8. Ericksonian Monographs 7. New York: Brunner-Mazel.

————. 1991. *Putting Difference to Work.* New York: Norton.

de Shazer, S., and I. Berg. 1985. "A Part Is Not Apart: Working with Only One of the Partners Present." In *Casebook of Marital Therapy,* ed. A. Gurman. New York: Guilford.

————. 1988. "Constructing Solutions." *The Family Therapy Networker* 12 (5): 42-43.

de Shazer, S., I Berg, E. Lipchik, E. Nunnally, A. Molnar, W. Gingerich, and M. Weiner-Davis. 1986. "Brief Therapy: Focused Solution Development." *Family Process* 25 (2): 207-222.

Gingerich, W. J., and S. de Shazer. 1991. "The BRIEFER Project: Using Expert Systems as Theory Construction Tools." *Family Process* 30 (2): 241-250.

Kowalski, K., and R. Kral. 1989. "The Geometry of Solution: Using the Scaling Technique." *Family Therapy Case Studies* 4 (1): 59-66.

Kral, R. 1986. "Indirect Therapy in the Schools." In *The Family Therapy Collections: Indirect Approaches in Family Therapy,* ed. S. de Shazer and R. Kral. Aspen: Rockville, MD.

————. 1992. "Solution-Focused Brief Therapy: Application in the Schools." In *Handbook of Family School Problems and Interventions: Systems Perspectives,* ed. M. J. Fine and C. I. Carlson, 330-346. New York: Allyn and Bacon.

Lankton, S., and C. Lankton. 1983. *The Answer Within: Clinical Framework of Ericksonian Hypnosis.* New York: Brunner-Mazel.

Lipchik, E. 1988a. "The Treatment of Disturbed Parent-Child Relationships." In *Troubled Relationships,* ed. E. W. Nunnally, C. S. Chilman, and F. M. Cox, 117-140. Families in Trouble Series, vol. 3. Newbury Park, CA: Sage.

————. 1988b. "Purposeful Sequence for Beginning the Solution-Focused Interview." In *Family Therapy Collections: Interviewing,* ed. E. Lipchik. Aspen: Rockville, MD.

Lipchik, E., and S. de Shazer. 1986. "The Purposeful Interview." *Journal of Strategic and Systemic Therapy* 5 (1-2): 88-99.

Lipchik, E., and D. Vega. 1985. "A Case Study from Two Perspectives." *Journal of Strategic and Systemic Therapy* 4 (3): 27-41.

Miller, S., and I. Berg. 1991. "Working with the Problem Drinker: A Solution-Focused Approach." *Arizona Counseling Journal* 16 (1): 3-12.

Molnar, A., and S. de Shazer. 1987. "Solution-Focused Therapy: Toward the Identification of Therapeutic Tasks." *Journal of Marital and Family Therapy* 13 (4): 349-358.

Walter, J., and J. Peller. 1992. *Becoming Solution-Focused in Brief Therapy.* New York: Brunner-Mazel.

Weiner-Davis, M., S. de Shazer, and W. Gingerich. 1987. "Building on Pretreatment Change to Construct the Therapeutic Solution: An Exploratory Study." *Journal of Marital and Family Therapy* 13 (4): 359-364.

A. J. Chevalier received her M.Ed. in Child Development and Family Relations from the University of North Carolina at Greensboro and her Ph.D. in Marriage and Family Therapy from Virginia Tech, and she has taught at Indiana University, Fairfield University, and Texas Woman's University. Her recent publications include *What If: Daily Throughts for Those Who Worry Too Much* (Health Communications, 1995). A practicing artist, Ajakai owns and operates Seven Stones Studio, a gallery and multidisciplinary center for the study of healing traditions in Buffalo, Wyoming.

Other New Harbinger Self-Help Titles

On the Clients Path: A Manual for the Practice of Solution-Focused Therapy, $39.95
Letting Go of Anger: The 10 Most Common Anger Styles and What to Do About Them, $12.95
Messages: The Communication Skills Workbook, Second Edition, $13.95
Coping With Chronic Fatigue Syndrome: Nine Things You Can Do, $12.95
The Anxiety & Phobia Workbook, Second Edition, $15.95
Thueson's Guide to Over-The Counter Drugs, $13.95
Natural Women's Health: A Guide to Healthy Living for Women of Any Age, $13.95
I'd Rather Be Married: Finding Your Future Spouse, $13.95
The Relaxation & Stress Reduction Workbook, Fourth Edition, $14.95
Living Without Depression & Manic Depression: A Workbook for Maintaining Mood Stability, $14.95
Belonging: A Guide to Overcoming Loneliness, $13.95
Coping With Schizophrenia: A Guide For Families, $13.95
Visualization for Change, Second Edition, $13.95
Postpartum Survival Guide, $13.95
Angry All The Time: An Emergency Guide to Anger Control, $12.95
Couple Skills: Making Your Relationship Work, $13.95
Handbook of Clinical Psychopharmacology for Therapists, $39.95
The Warrior's Journey Home: Healing Men, Healing the Planet, $13.95
Weight Loss Through Persistence, $13.95
Post-Traumatic Stress Disorder: A Complete Treatment Guide, $39.95
Stepfamily Realities: How to Overcome Difficulties and Have a Happy Family, $13.95
Leaving the Fold: A Guide for Former Fundamentalists and Others Leaving Their Religion, $13.95
Father-Son Healing: An Adult Son's Guide, $12.95
The Chemotherapy Survival Guide, $11.95
Your Family/Your Self: How to Analyze Your Family System, $12.95
Being a Man: A Guide to the New Masculinity, $12.95
The Deadly Diet, Second Edition: Recovering from Anorexia & Bulimia, $11.95
Last Touch: Preparing for a Parent's Death, $11.95
Consuming Passions: Help for Compulsive Shoppers, $11.95
Self-Esteem, Second Edition, $13.95
Depression & Anxiety Management: An audio tape for managing emotional problems, $11.95
I Can't Get Over It, A Handbook for Trauma Survivors, $13.95
Concerned Intervention, When Your Loved One Won't Quit Alcohol or Drugs, $11.95
Redefining Mr. Right, $11.95
Dying of Embarrassment: Help for Social Anxiety and Social Phobia, $12.95
The Depression Workbook: Living With Depression and Manic Depression, $14.95
Risk-Taking for Personal Growth: A Step-by-Step Workbook, $14.95
The Marriage Bed: Renewing Love, Friendship, Trust, and Romance, $11.95
Focal Group Psychotherapy: For Mental Health Professionals, $44.95
Hot Water Therapy: Save Your Back, Neck & Shoulders in 10 Minutes a Day $11.95
Older & Wiser: A Workbook for Coping With Aging, $12.95
Prisoners of Belief: Exposing & Changing Beliefs that Control Your Life, $10.95
Be Sick Well: A Healthy Approach to Chronic Illness, $11.95
Men & Grief: A Guide for Men Surviving the Death of a Loved One., $12.95
When the Bough Breaks: A Helping Guide for Parents of Sexually Abused Childern, $11.95
Love Addiction: A Guide to Emotional Independence, $12.95
When Once Is Not Enough: Help for Obsessive Compulsives, $13.95
The New Three Minute Meditator, $12.95
Getting to Sleep, $12.95
Beyond Grief: A Guide for Recovering from the Death of a Loved One, $13.95
Thoughts & Feelings: The Art of Cognitive Stress Intervention, $13.95
Leader's Guide to the Relaxation & Stress Reduction Workbook, Fourth Edition, $19.95
The Divorce Book, $11.95
Hypnosis for Change: A Manual of Proven Techniques, 2nd Edition, $13.95
The Chronic Pain Control Workbook, $14.95
My Parent's Keeper: Adult Children of the Emotionally Disturbed, $11.95
When Anger Hurts, $13.95
Free of the Shadows: Recovering from Sexual Violence, $12.95
Lifetime Weight Control, $11.95
Love and Renewal: A Couple's Guide to Commitment, $13.95
The Habit Control Workbook, $12.95

Call **toll free, 1-800-748-6273**, to order. Have your Visa or Mastercard number ready. Or send a check for the titles you want to New Harbinger Publications, Inc., 5674 Shattuck Avenue, Oakland, CA 94609. Include $3.80 for the first book and 75¢ for each additional book, to cover shipping and handling. (California residents please include appropriate sales tax.) Allow four to six weeks for delivery.

Prices subject to change without notice.